Blessed with Evil

Blessed with Evil

✦

A Story of the Hell's Angels and the Evil Spirits Motorcycle Clubs

Parco Senia

iUniverse, Inc.
New York Lincoln Shanghai

Blessed with Evil

A Story of the Hell's Angels and the Evil Spirits Motorcycle Clubs

iUniverse books may be ordered through booksellers or by contacting:

iUniverse
2021 Pine Lake Road, Suite 100
Lincoln, NE 68512
www.iuniverse.com
1-800-Authors (1-800-288-4677)

Because of the dynamic nature of the Internet, any Web addresses or links contained in this book may have changed since publication and may no longer be valid.

The views expressed in this work are solely those of the author and do not necessarily reflect the views of the publisher, and the publisher hereby disclaims any responsibility for them.

ISBN: 978-0-595-45969-8 (pbk)
ISBN: 978-0-595-90270-5 (ebk)

Printed in the United States of America

Contents

come storming in club to close shop-a false warning—A Lawrence cop trying to bribe me on false pretense-rape—My poem-Life in General—

Introduction

Blessed with Evil tells the story of the life and times of two outlaw motorcycle clubs, the Hell's Angels and the Evil Spirits and I as a member in New England from the early seventies to the present. It is an extraordinary depiction of the underground scene of the motorcycle lifestyle, chronicling the parties, stunts, stabbings, rumbles, women, drugs, arrests, and the journey through the legal system ending in jail and death. My own near-death experience brought me to an understanding that the richness of life lies from within.

This motorcycle book is an action pack type thrilling story of a life that only a few people lead, but many are curious about, a life of "living on the edge". The total monthly audience for *Easyriders* magazine which we got photographed and printed in 74 is close to 3.5 million readers today. I still cream over the magazine, just kidding. I grew into becoming a loner after my brain surgery, this way the healing process would take care of its own, an outlaw on his own! I had to do it my way. I worked for the public sector as an independent. The only difference is a law man steals for his increase and glamour, while the outlaw steals for survival. {"All I'm saying is, be an outlaw … but do it your own way."—Hunter S Thompson, July 6, 1967}

1

Dysfunctional From the Start

The first traumatic experience I can recall as coming aware in this world was the age of three years old. It was when my mother placed my brother and myself over my grandparents to live when she left my father. My mother went to live with her sister. I literally shit my pants and started crying. My grandmother cleaned it up. I can't recall any of my childhood before that time. It must have been a serious traumatic event to me. I can't recall how long we lived there, but I believe it was close to a year.

I was born in the city of Lawrence, Massachusetts. My father started a restaurant business in the city of Lowell, Mass. I was brought up in an eight room house in the town of Methuen, close to the Lawrence line. This area is well known as the Merrimack Valley.

By the time I was in first grade, my family was back together again but not all the time. My mother still left us on and off to live with her sisters or brothers. It had a lot to do with my father's business. He owned a restaurant and we were all part of the woodwork of the business. By the time I was in sixth grade, I was already out on the streets with my other greaser buddies. If not there, I'd be at the restaurant.

I got into playing drums and a couple of my friends played guitars. We got into forming a band which we named the Midnight Riders. We played a lot of Mitch Ryder and the Detroit Wheels' tunes. When the seventh grade came along, I was already getting drunk and high, joy riding in hot cars. We were breaking into houses for whatever we could use, alcohol, money or whatever would float our boat. This was with the other fellows I met during that time. They were from divorced families themselves. It was all too bizarre to believe. The guys who I played with in the band came from typical families.

One of them, a tight friend, was dysfunctional despite that his family was together. I would sleep over his place on weekends. When his parents would go to bed, we would climb out of the bedroom window and be out and about with the scene on Broadway. We were too cool to be true. Our band entered the seventh grade talent show and won first prize. There was another band competing with us and they played the psychedelic music. We stuck to the good old rock'n roll. By the eighth grade I became an official juvenile delinquent.

One of my friends and I decided to co-opt my father's car to go to the local amusement park. The car was available since my father drove a pick-up truck to work at the restaurant. We got busted by the police, while leaving rubber after a red light. We had to attend juvenile court. My father made me stay in my room for a weekend as punishment. After that, I did one more breaking and entering into a house with the guys, but I was too paranoid so I decided to give it up.

By the beginning of my high school years, I owned a 100 c.c. Bridgestone motorcycle. There were trails in the woods right behind the restaurant. During the slow periods of work in the middle of the afternoon, I'd be able to go out trail riding for a couple of hours. It was a gas to itself and it was more fun than I expected. Then I'd be back at the business for the supper rush.

My first year of high school was one that I'd never forget. After school the guys and I would set up a football game to let our oats out. One day I headed to the playground to get into a game. Sure enough the guys were asking for blood. They wanted to play tackle not tag. I held back, telling them "No way! I have white chinos on." I didn't want to get them ruined with grass stains on them. They were disappointed but finally agreed to play tag. We were crazy anyway playing without any head gear. Well, the game was being won by my team when the other side started yelling "Tackle!" We finally agreed. The next thing you know, death introduced itself to me. I was tackling one of the guys. While I was on my knees, one of the guys on my team ran in to help me bring him down. At the same time, his knee contacted my temple on the right side and knocked me for a loop. I had a fractured skull along with a punctured ear drum. I went into a coma.

Coming out of that wasn't easy. The doctors thought that I might become a vegetable. I came to within twenty four hours. I was seeing double, and I was deaf in my right ear. Lying down on the right side of my head was like lying on a wall of jagged rocks. I'd be sedated with a shot of morphine. I was able to make it out of the hospital within a few weeks. But I was still seeing double and deaf in the ear. They had to wait for the fracture to heal before they could operate to restore my hearing. I also had to constantly steer my eyes to the left in order to see straight and compensate for the double vision. Slowly but surely, my vision returned to normal. After the surgery everything seemed to work out successfully.

That was my first encounter with death. One step forward, two steps back. It was life in the fast lane so to speak, the mystical law of cause and effect.

When I turned sixteen and was able to get my automobile license, I bought a '65 Harley Sportster. Before my last year of high school, all hell broke loose between my father and me over the restaurant business. I left the business and my home. My sister and her husband offered me a room to sleep and to live with them. It was just a doorway to my crazy drug infested outlaw days.

I was the only pot dealer in high school. My closest friends in class were Rick, Russ, and another biker friend, Butch who was a year ahead of me. I'd get stoned on Seconals over Rick's place listening to the Jeff Beck Group. We'd be in a nod while listening to the tunes. It would be time for me to leave before his mother would be home from work. I'd head back to my sister's place to grab another bag of weed which I had stashed. Then it would be off to Butchie's pad, where he lived with his ol'lady. I'd be getting stoned with them for the rest of the evening. One day at school, Rick, Russ and I dropped some LSD at lunch time. Russ would start to peak and I'd blow his mind, telling him there was a spider on his shoulder during class. He would be laughing, then get up from his desk and start running down the hall. I'd go chase him to get him back to the classroom. It was a vocational high school so it was all male instructors. The teacher knew we were on something, but he didn't press on us. It was some experience. I was the only student to graduate in dungarees. That evening, I headed up the beach tripping on Windowpane acid. A group of the classmates were up there throwing a party at the Reservation Camping Park. The next morning I'd be back home working on my Harley. It was some time in the early seventies, believe me.

It was a hot sunny summer afternoon. I was strolling around Lawrence when Snake, a French Canadian biker friend, pulled up beside me and started a conversation. We had become good friends during the last Laconia, New Hampshire bike run. I made it up there to party without my bike since it was going through a complete overhaul. I ended up going there by foot or bust with a sleeping bag over my shoulder and my thumb out in front of the highway. Another biker pulled over and invited me to come along to a private get-away party, not far from the main drag. That's where all the partying and action was.

We arrived. There were about a dozen cabins full of bikers. Music was playing. There were drinks and smoke available too. But I was getting a little irritable since I knew the real deal was out on Route 106.

After spending a few hours at the cabins, I wanted to see where the live action was. I was young and curious. The year was 1973 and I was graduating out of high school, where I had majored in auto mechanics. As I trucked along the highway, bikes were roaring along by the dozens. They must have been going on 'til four in the morning. I could see the dawn first stirrings coming up over the mountains. Snake and a few other bikers were camping out along the highway and as I approached, he asked me to come and join the party. We started shooting the shit. J.P., Fabian and Snake all wanted to get to know me better. We talked about Canada, bikes, and whatever crossed our minds as the dawn continued to break. We decided to get some shut-eye for a few hours.

It was starting to get a little nippy. I was in my sleeping bag, trying to stay warm by wiggling closer and closer to the campfire. It was getting warmer and the bottom of the sleeping bag felt peculiarly warmer. I woke up with a flash and in a panic! The sleeping bag had caught fire!!! I put out the fire immediately by stomping it with my hands. It was pretty funny when you come right down to it, camping out and getting a little "burnt" in the process.

By mid-morning the bikers were all roaring down the highway, showing off the power they had riding between their legs. I got on the back of Snake's machine as we went riding down the strip with all the other machines on parade. Snake had me swallowing my balls as he lifted his bike off the ground. He lifted it so high I was surprised he didn't lose the machine. He repeated it over a half dozen times. Man, it was a feeling no one could describe being on that bike.

Sometimes I get fuckin' disgusted with life. Sometimes I wonder if it's all worth it. Well let me tell you something—take what you can get because life is too short. That I know. Life is a never-ending freeway, filled with obstacles, intersections, exits and the occasional enlightenment. I do care about Buddha, balance, and the middle way. But I'm not going to get into this philosophical shit. It all ends up the same, Nirvana, The Way.

It was The Mystical Enlightenment, Everything, and yet Nothing too. But right now let's turn the page and return to the year 1973.

I was already out on my own, riding a 65 Harley Davidson. The drug culture was already at its peak, and I was more or less at the half-way point. Sex, drugs, rock & roll, and naturally, motorcycles were the going way of living for me.

The people I hung around with mainly were biker freaks. Or then again, some were just freak freaks. The beginning of the seventies was the thresh hold of the American Dream.

The Vietnam War helped crush the era of the beat generation, and we were the ones that got beaten. It all seems like government propaganda. It helped divide the population of our generation so that blue and white collar authorities would hold power over the so-called "hippie new age" youth and supposedly bring the economy back.

Some of us fought the war, beat the draft, or waited impatiently, wondering whether or not we would be called to the line of duty. Drugs and the drug culture helped curb the worry. Everything was for the here and now, living on the edge.

2

Evil Spirits Arise

The guys I rode and partied with were a mixed crowd. Some were local, while others were from Canada. There was Butchie, Arty, Dougie, John. They were all from Merrimack Valley. Along with Dude, Tonto, Jumpin' Jack, Captain Video, Wilkie, Quick Nick, Lenny, Rebel, Geronamo, Zap, and Preacher. The guys from Canada were Snake, J.P., Norman, Fabian, Jean, Jill, Ronnie and Julian.

Snake and I decided to form a club. He knew of one already operating in Canada called the "Evil Spirits." I knew where the Hell's Angels were located. We decided to form a chapter of the "Spirits" in Massachusetts, but first had to haul up to Canada to forge the alliance with the main chapter. On our way up to the border we passed a potato truck at a yellow line in Presque Isle, Maine. At six in the morning, dressed in dungaree vest cut-offs and jeans, long-hair, we just stood out like a sore thumb in contrast to the old school hicks in Maine. The local police are just dying to have a little action at that time in the morning. After all, they have to have something out there in the sticks to make their day.

We ended up getting pulled over. Since we looked so felonious, they radioed the border patrol to come down and check us out thoroughly. We had been on the road for about seven hours, stoned out to the gills, and still had some speed to consume while completing our journey.

While we were waiting for the big man to arrive, Fabian was smart enough to put his speed in his stocking. Luckily, the local cop standing over us didn't notice what Fabian had done. I was so wired I just left my stash in my pocket. Well, was that ever a problem? The border patrol arrived, pulled us out of the car, frisked us, and went and found my speed. That was it. Snake, J.P., Fabian and I got hauled into the station where we were just about completely stripped searched. Sure enough, Fabian's bag of speed fell out of his stocking. Curtains! Dragnet! We wound up being placed in the Houlton County Jail for a preliminary hearing. I was seventeen, so they placed me in minimum security.

The female jail was adjacent to my cell block. Some dude that was going on work release was placed down the hall from me. He could at least see the women from his tier to their window. I got to talking to a girl named Molly. We formed some communication by passing letters to each other by coat hanger, pushing and pulling, to and from, under her door. Cy, the prison guard, caught on to us one time, and he stated that if I kept it up, he would have to move me to another cell further down the tier. We still kept on passing letters.

The inmate who was on work release gave the women a free show one evening. He pulled out his prick and whipped it around a bit. The female inmates enjoyed every minute of it. I could hear them laughing in amazement. The dude had a sizable sausage to slab around with.

After a couple of weeks rolled by, Fabian and I got to make it to the court house. Previously, Snake was at our arraignment the first Monday morning after we got stopped and busted. He had the date of the hearing so he could contact my mother to let her know what was up with me. My sister drove up my mother for the hearing. It came down to a hundred dollar fine and off we went. Fabian was convicted of a possession charge, since he was over eighteen. I was able to escape without a record hanging over my head.

The ride home was long, but comfortable through the state of Maine. When we made it back to Massachusetts, it was a relief knowing we would be home within an hour. We dropped Fabian off at his apartment. I finally made it back to my comfortable bedroom. There's no place like home Mama.

The next day, it was time to take my Harley Sportster for a ride. It fired up without any problems. I rode to Fabian's to go for a quick run together on our scoots, basically around the city. While we were passing an intersection down-town, we collided side to side with each other. Fabian landed on his ass. I was able to keep my bike afloat. We were laughing with each other, knowing how great it felt to be free again after the Canadian Border ordeal.

Snake, J.P., Fabian, Preacher and I decided to go up to Ste-Rose, Canada, to begin working on getting our Massachusetts chapter started.

We finally made it across the border and received our colors from the main chapter. It was one hell of a party from the start of the trip to the ride back to the States. When we arrived, the president said that he would have the clubhouse parking lot plowed out and wood in the fireplace within an hour. The brothers up in Canada were really great people. Their ol'ladies sewed our colors on for us while we were up there.

Our third journey up to Canada turned out to be a real trip. When we got over the border, the snow was really coming down in blizzard conditions. They must have had at least three feet of snow already on the ground. Snake was driving his 66 Chevy Impala without any snow tires. When we got past the border, it was all country, hills and valleys. Snake would just keep the gas pedal to the floor. We would be floating over hill tops on a wing and a prayer. To him, it was a normal way of driving in Canada during the winter season. After traveling so many miles, we would get to the top of a hill and halt to take a break and spark up a joint. Lighten up the load so to speak.

When we would attempt to roll on back on the road, the heat from the rear tires would cause the ice from underneath them to melt. They would embed in the ice. Butchie was in a cast from his last motorcycle accident. We'd try to get rolling, but the tires would just spin deeper into the ice. J.P., Butchie and I would get out of the car and try to rock the vehicle to get it out of the ruts. The snow was really coming down. We couldn't budge the car. Luckily a snow plow was coming up the hill. The driver got the truck behind us and gave us a push. Off and rolling we went for a few miles. Snake made it to the top of one of the hills and decided to take another break to blow another bone. Sure enough when we tried to take off, the same thing happened as before. We couldn't get the Chevy rolling again by pushing it.

We got back into the car. The plow truck was coming up the hill, only this time the driver went right by us. I guess that if we were foolish enough to stop again, we'd have to pay the price indeed! We got back out of the car and began rocking it again. Faithfully we were able to get the Chevy rolling out of the rut we were in. We hopped back into the car and off we went. We passed the plow truck winding along the hills and valleys, finally making it into the town of Ste-Rose.

We were awfully frozen sitting in the back seat for eight hours without any heat. My feet were like ice blocks! We landed at the president's estate where he had a fancy, heated, in-ground swimming pool, contained within its own special plexiglas enclosure. He was Snake's cousin, Gil, whose father owned a construction company, and was one of the richest men in the city. Gil lost a limb in a ski-mobile accident. He was very calm and collected. If I had his fortune, I probably would be too. After we thawed out, we went down to their clubhouse. It was located on an acre of land in a wooded area of the city. He told us he would have it all plowed out with wood in the fireplace within an hour. We got a few z's in the car while we waited for the log cabin to be open.

Once everything got into order the party began. The members up there were really great guys. I hung around with a member named Bernie and his ol'lady. They could hardly understand English, but we were able to communicate with each other. When the evening arrived, we would head out to a dance club to party. On our way into the club, we almost had a jam with some rednecks that started mouthing off at us. We let it pass. The night went on pretty good and the band sang all in English. The French Canadian women were gorgeous, especially Bernie's ol'lady. When we got back to the clubhouse, we would party the night away.

It was a great vacation all and all. The ride back home went much smoother than the ride we had up. There wasn't even any snow on the ground when we got to Massachusetts.

Everything seemed to run synchronized, faster then you would consider what cause and effect could do, and all in progression so to speak. We decided to hold our meetings over at Ronnie's apartment. Not all who I mentioned became members. Then again some that I haven't mentioned came into the club sooner or later.

I got the position as Road Captain. I'd set up all the runs and set up the parties too. I pressed to all the brothers at a meeting that we had to get affiliated with the Hell's Angels. It was the right thing to do so we wouldn't be a Mickey Mouse type of club. This way, we'd be in tune with all the scheduled events and be recognized.

We had a hang-around club named Don's Manor on Broadway and the French Social Club was not even a mile away. We were either working on or riding our scoots, or partying with some cute babes, fucked up on either THC-LSD-Methamphetamine-downs-weed-and-alcohol of choice. On a cool fall night, I would be getting a wicked good buzz on, just peaking on acid, and would decide to go out and fire up my scoot and take it for it for a quick run around the city. Between the vibes, the rushes, the purr of the V-Twin, the exhaust pipes would be crackling all in one steady motion. I would decide to bang a few gears, all hell would break loose. By the time I'd make it back to the club, everything would be flowing in perseverance. The acid would not be part of me, but completely me.

3

Heading for the Big Times

The Angels would come down and party with us or vice versa, we'd go to them. Wherever we were, it turned out to be a real gas. Members such as Mousey, Deacon, Tom-Tom, Shakey, R.B., Whiskey George, Dirty Dave, Suave Dave, Hawkeye, Fuck-Up, and Hook from the Lowell chapter were tightly associated with us. We had other connections with the Salem and Lynn chapters with Buster, Billy, Big Al, Harpy, and Hoppy, along with members from out-of-state chapters. It turned out to be a life in the fast lane so to speak, living on the edge. So I decided to live it, Damn it!

I started seeing some kinky broad who was really spaced out. One evening when I was out partying with her, we decided to go back to her place. I dropped her off then went to find a place to park. By the time I parked and made it to her door, she wouldn't answer. Not only was I stoned, but I was pissed. I had an idea that she was on the hard stuff—the big H, so I was just playing along with her, hoping that eventually I'd get into her pants. One night when I was down Don's Manor shooting some pool with a couple of Angel's, Deacon and Tom-Tom, along with my bros, I decided to take a ride to her place to see what was happening. I knocked on her door. No answer. As I walked out of the hallway down to the street level, she was just approaching the stairway porch with another broad and two dudes. They seemed to be dealers to me. One grabbed me in a full nelson, while another started swinging punches at me. One said to the other, "We're taking him with us". Luckily Jean was passing by in his Plymouth Cuda. I yelled, "Hey, Jean!" and he jammed on his brakes and threw his car into reverse. The dude that was throwing the punches ran out after him with a "piece" in his hand. I was able to break away from the dude that held me, headed to my car, reaching for a set of nunchakus sticks. But no go—they weren't where I thought they were. I hopped into my car and had split back to the bar. "Come On, I Need Help!" I gathered Snake, J.P., and Fabian. I was bleeding from the nose. Deacon and Tom-Tom looked in surprise wondering what the fuck was going on.

When the bros and I got back to her place, the mutha-fuckers split. We left her pad in shambles, letting them know who they were fucking with. I don't know if they were out to kill me or hold me for ransom. It was some bizarre encounter. The detectives pulled us over and gave me the lowdown that I was shot at while heading back to the bar. They couldn't keep up with me as I threw a bullshit line at them. It was back to the bar for a few brews and the closing of the night.

As time went on, we kept on partying it up at Don's Manor. Tom-Tom and Deacon came by for a Friday night out. The juke box was blaring, the pool table was occupied, and women were at the bar.

Tom-Tom decided to put his coins on the pool table. A couple of chicks started making time with him while he waited to get in on playing some. He finally got his turn, gliding along like he was putting on a show, hardly missing any shots, until Don, the owner of the club, almost walked into Tom's stick while he was making a shot. A confrontation started. Don had a hair across his ass since it was his bar. We were really disappointed with him, since we were the ones bringing in all the business. We decided to head to the French Social Club, live band on weekends, but it seemed like a bad night all around. The manager came down on Deacon, stating that he didn't want any colors in the club. They never came down on us, but the Hell's Angels was a whole different ball game. Deacon was bullshit. He came down with his constitutional rights, freedom of expression and the right to privacy. He did it nice and cunningly, we were able to hang in there to closing. It was just another night out in the city.

We kept all the good times happening at the French Social Club because the weekends there were one hell of a trip. On weekends the club escalated to over a hundred patrons. The live band was one hell of a group. The female gender was always ready to get up to boogie to the music. A lot of the gals were from Canada. Some were locals from the city, basically hanging with us. "*We don't smoke marijuana at the French Social, we don't take our trips on LSD*," the band played on. The singer would grin at me like, "Yeah, Right, tell me another one." I'd grin back, tripping my ever-lovin-mutha-fuckin' brains out. On a crisp autumn night, I'd be peaking on some really good acid, leave the club, get on my machine for a nice fuckin' ride. At closing time, something would come about. A bite to chow down, get a buzz on, go for a nice ride, pussy to fuck with, or all of the above. It was a way of life, a way to be who you were. If you didn't know already, eventually you would find your path, as the Grateful Dead sang, "*What a long, strange trip it's been.*"

The club started to escalate. Hang-arounds, prospects, and members came and went. Some of the prospects took advantage of their colors, not coming to meetings and so on. When that happened, we'd take their patch back. Then a new hang-around type would come along and try to become a prospect. It was a vicious circle.

We had a member who knew of an owner of an old biker bar that was closed in the late sixties. At that time, there was a biker club called G.L.M.A. which stood for the Greater Lawrence Motorcycle Association and they operated the bar. We got the chance to re-open it. It was a blessing in disguise. The *"Evil Spirits"* blossomed on us. The name of the bar was the Calumet Club and it turned out to be a home away from home. We had *Broadway* by the *Balls!* The club had two sides—one for the public, the other private, such as for meetings, bike repairs, stag parties, and so on. We had access to the back yard. On a hot summer night, we'd go out and get stoned and shoot the shit. The Angels would come down and party on a regular basis.

One hot afternoon, the Lowell chapter arrived with a couple of New York members. I noticed their rough and toughness just by looking at them. One of them got rolling with a half-dozen shots of tequila. "These are naughty sticks." He struck his nunchakus sticks on the hard core wooden realm of the bar. "For anyone who's nodding out...." *Crack!* There was another slam to the bar. "... Anyone not in with us?" *Bam-Slam-Crack!* He caught everyone's attention. After a couple more shots, he put his eye on Norman's ol'lady. He wound up blowing his gourd, "I want that gal for myself." Rachel got very paranoid and stayed behind Norman who didn't want to get into any confrontation. "Let's fight for her ass!" the Angel stated. Luckily, the Lowell Angels got in the middle to break up the confrontation and held the member back from throwing the first punch. What a Mutha-Fuckin' afternoon! Everything cooled down. If you ever party with over a half-dozen Angels, you'll know what I'm talking about. After that, Norman turned in his colors. He didn't want anything to do with the flying colors of an outlaw motorcycle club. No blame. Norman was a good shit.

4

The Brothers

Snake was one of the most extraordinary brothers I've ever known. He was the first elected president of the club, since it was both of us that started the club. Before I met him, he went through a devastating head-on collision on his scoot with some cager. Many bones were broken in his body. He had some shanks and pins placed in his damaged bone structures. You could tell that he was like a fuse permanently lit waiting to explode. He was *"Blessed with Evil"* but still one with his head screwed on straight. One of our friends, Julian, a French-Canadian, had a hair across his ass with Snake from way back. He would lash out and start a beef at an unexpected time and we'd break it up. He'd make it up, months later, the same shit would happen. They'd be arguing in French, so I never knew what the bullshit was all about.

One night while we were partying, Snake was out riding with another biker along with a couple of babes from the club. He knew how to get on his machine. Man did he fly, until that night. He slid over a sewer cover so fast that the bike dumped on the poor bastard. He went down with the machine, right underneath a parked vehicle. The chick he was riding broke her leg. He almost lost his foot. It actually twisted around like a corkscrew. All the bros were in total dismay on the issue. Buddy the bar owner lined up the bros with free brews 'til further word came on what the outcome would be. It fucked up Snake totally. He was crazier than ever. You could imagine another near fatal encounter. He was in and out of the hospital for surgery for about a year. At first the doctors didn't know whether or not they were going to keep the foot from being amputated. He eventually had a shank inserted in the ankle so he would be able to walk with less of a limp.

Snake and I had a lot of wild times together, especially when we would trip together on some hallucinatory type drug. He'd blow your mind just trying to follow him. One night we were installing some stereo equipment in his car while we were getting off on serious shit. By the time we got it all together, we'd be peaking on the acid and lighting up a number to head out for a cruise. One of his

Canadian gals would be sitting between us. The music would be blaring. Man it would turn out to be a real trip.

Luckily, he had decent luck with women having off and on steady relations. He was egocentric. He ended up with a lot of obstacles. There is more to his story than can meet the eye. I'm just trying to give you a broader view of the *Spirits*, the mystery of their lifestyles and results that came forth from the here and now.

Butchie was not only the doctor of the club, but an artist. He had a lot of connections with the drug dealers. He became one himself. He would do business usually on Friday, pay day. There would be a knock on the door, a customer would pop in, and the deal would go through. When business was completed for the evening, it would be our turn to get a high on some pure Methamphetamine. Once we were high, he'd put on his favorite tune, "*Long Distance*" by Yes.

When it came to art, he'd be the one to see for a custom paint-job on your bike. We'd be speeding our brains out. It would be about three in the morn. We'd head to his garage to throw a couple of coats of clear on a certain machine, smoking some weed in between coats. Everything was a profession with him. He was one of my tightest bros.

Before the club started, Butch and Artie had their own pad. We'd party and ride together. They had connections with other bikers, when I needed some mechanical work or advice, they would be there. I got to know some of the best. They had an Alaskan Husky named Parco who got hit and killed by a cager. The name got passed on to me—"*Parco*." It stuck to me to this day.

Before the club days, we'd go up to Jeff's Custom Shop in Haverhill to hang, shoot the shit, smoke a number. Jeff had an Angel from Lowell as a mechanic named Shakey Al. Man was he a hot shit. It was a hell of a pastime. We'd check out some custom parts, ordered a few, get on our scoots and split. Butch always had a live-in ol'lady in the making. He was one, such as me, to associate with the Hell's Angels more than the other members.

Butch did so much speed I felt like an amateur when it came to getting off on the stuff. He would always have the downs to crash with. He had a birthday party over his place for me one year. We started on some *acid*, being followed by some heavy drink and some high grade weed. I felt like I was comatose on an alcoholic trip, tripping on the acid. I had to drive my girlfriend back to her place after the party ended. When I made it back to Butchie's pad, just about everyone had split. That's how fast the night went by. He decided to call me into the kitchen to do some power booster—methamphetamine. I became straight in a matter of seconds.

Jumpin Jack Flash was one hell of a character. He could talk his head off faster then his Greyhound dog could run the quarter-mile lap. I met Jack when I was going out with his next door neighbor, Linda. Linda was originally from Stockton, California and what a dynamite chick she was. I guess she knew it. I loved the babe, especially when she would ask me if I wanted a blowjob. The Flash was always wheeling and dealing, he was a THC freak, along with hash and weed. He had a good friend named Captain Video. This guy was really cool. He was right up there with current affairs. We would all be sitting at the kitchen table, smoking a bowl stuffed with hash and THC. The Captain would start rambling on about politics, current affairs, and corporate affairs. It would expand my conscience to a higher perception in life. The night would roll on. Jack would have the music playing. Snake would lay back on the carpeted floor, listening to the music, *"Rocket Man burning out his fuse up here alone."* Everything was cool, I mean really cool.

Jack's ol'lady was a professional shoplifter, from the clothing stores to the grocery stores. She was something else. He had a 305 Honda Dream for an emergency back-up. We called it *"The Batmobile."* It was a real rat, but it served its purpose. Jack was never in the same place for more than six hours, unless he was in the rack. He'd be here-there-nowhere, all at the same time. He was a crazy fucker.

One night, Jack, J.P., Snake, and I decided to make a night out up in Newburyport at the Black Sheep Lounge. The music was playing and everyone was having a good time. Out of the unexpected, Jack flipped right the fuck out. I mean the man just blew a short circuit. He started throwing chairs around, flipping the tables over, whatever he could get his hands on. Some people didn't know whether we were out to cause trouble or what. We noticed he was foaming at the mouth. All we knew was we had to get him the fuck out of there. When we got him in the van, he went into a complete seizure. We headed back to Lawrence, on the way we stopped at a bar to cool our jets while we would take turns staying in the van 'til he became conscious. We guessed he was out of it on all the drugs he was ingesting. He finally came to or we would have got him to a hospital. That was Jack, here today, gone tomorrow.

Preacher was one of a kind. Nothing seemed to ever bother him. I guess that's how he got the name Preacher. He was always available for almost any situation-runs-parties-meetings-even the extraordinary. He was a former Vietnam vet, hard core, but always carried a shit-eating grin. He rode a chopped rigid Triumph with a springer front-end about 16 inches extended. When he rode by the Calumet, he would pull one hell of a wheelie, then return back to the bar and head for a brew.

He was a party animal, just like the other bros. At one stag party that we threw, Preacher participated with the stripper. He dropped his pants and started chasing her around with his *dick* swinging in his hand. I was popping in and out of the party since I was preoccupied with my scoot along with some babe. It was all and all a great night. I caught the best part of the show being Preacher and the prostitute, killing two birds with one stone.

Some nights we would get so wasted. The club would be closing. We would take a ride up towards the mountains on a cold autumn night. It would be due to the Angel Dust we smoked all night that would keep us afloat, feeling like jelly, to the early hours of the morning. By then, there would be snow squalls hovering around the mountains, nothing that would last. By the time we would make it back, the bros would be planning a noon time run along the river, up to the beach with a few pit stops on the way back to have a few brews.

Preacher's wife was a decent ol'lady. She never interfered with club business, or his either. His son was a really good kid. He was like a nephew to me. We played Batman and Robin together to pass time before a weekly meeting took place.

Dude started coming down to the Calumet. He impressed me with his lifestyle and experience. He wanted to become a member and would do anything to get that status. I had a prospect which I wasn't really impressed with. Colors were on hold since we were having more manufactured. I told my prospect that if he wanted to keep his colors, he'd have to go a round with Dude fair and square. Dude agreed. They both went at it. The prospect went into a wrestling match and got the best of Dude. The minute he let up, Dude cold-cocked him right in the face. The fight ended as soon as he felt his power-house fist. Dude went crazy stating "*Ha-Ha! You lose! Ha-Ha-Ha!*" He was already a one percent outlaw as he'd done time in the past on some felonious rap. All and all he was a hot shit and had a lot of balls. He was also active in the Navy during the Vietnam era. When I made him a member, he had me throwing more punches trying to break in one of his prospects.

J.P. was some kind of women's man. He had pussy written all over his face, a smooth operator. He was a mellow, good natured type of brother. He had a righteous old fashioned type of shed in his back yard. It had enough room for two scoots, Coleman heater, tool box, radio, and a twelve pack. We'd spend the rebuild months on our scoots, tearing them down for the winter, customizing them with newer parts, paint jobs, and motor work. It was "*Zen And The Art Of Motorcycle Maintenance*" in a different perspective. Around supper time we'd close shop, clean up, chow down, and wait for Snake to come by to pick us up to go party at the bar for the evening. I used to love playing with his sister while waiting for J.P. to finish dabbling himself up. What a fuckin' doll she was, with her Canadian accent and her luscious body. I wouldn't let my eyes off her. I could hear her giggling as she passed me. Finally, J.P. would be all set to get up. Out the door we went. We'd have one hell of a good time. The Calumet Club was our home away from home.

Nick was the backbone of the club. That's how he got the name Quick Nick. He was always staying busy with his own shit or the club's bullshit. He was one crazy fucker. Nick had a neat step van that was used to travel and party in. We'd bring it on a run such as the Laconia bash in the early seventies, when it was just partying and camping on the highway. If it wasn't the support he gave to the club, it probably wouldn't have lasted as long as it did. When we lost our barroom, he was the guy that had the house to give to the club for our stomping grounds for a song and a dance. When we would go out and party together, we would always have a wild fuckin' time. He was the man.

5

Calumet Club

Our club got tighter than ever. More bikers would stop by to party and get a good buzz on. Let me put it this way, if any brother needed a place to crash, the door was open at the Calumet Club for him. One night I was with one of my gals. The house was rocking. Everything was going really smooth. A group of the Lowell Hell's Angels came down to tie a good one on. R.B. was a rugged type style outlaw with a good head on his shoulders. You could tell that he had been the route. He had a mellow type attitude, as long as you didn't cross him. That was like any other Angel. We started shooting the shit and having a few brews when he asked me if we could talk personally. So I brought him into the side room. With a serious look, he asked "What's your top priority in life right now?" With no delay I replied, "*Colors-Man-Colors*" with my thumb over my shoulder, pointing to them on my back. "Right on, Right on!" he said. "What about that female you're with? She open game or what?" he asked. "She's open game," I said. "Cool, let's go back and party," he smiled, putting his arm over my shoulder. He then went back to the other side of the bar and ordered a round. I was on one side of her, while he was on the other. We got into a good conversation, while he started to put the make on her. She was enthused with his style in the making. All the other brothers were partying it up with the other Angels. Some came on their bikes, others, in a car.

There was a strip joint not far from our place. Around midnight, some of the brothers convinced the Angels to head out for the club before last call. My lady friend got in the car with R.B. I was already half lit, hopping on my scoot with a couple of Angels by my side. Off we went. When we got to a rotary, my bike stalled out. I started pissing and moaning, yelling at the car behind us, "*Go the fuck around us!*"

Tom-Tom was right aside of me, "*Cool it, those are our bros!*" I looked back, gave my bike a shot on the kicker, and off we roared. We made it for the last show. It turned out to be a decent night, all in all. When the weekend rounded up, I contacted the gal I turned R.B. onto. She told me that he fast talked her into a piece of ass, or my ass was going to be grassed. It didn't bother me. I had already humped her!

The Calumet was rolling right along, like a hurricane. Well, not exactly, but close to it. Smoking some weed over there was like taking a leak in the toilet. It was always available. Nick came down on me one time for smoking a number in the side room. "For Christ sake Parco, some dick could be walking in here right now without us knowing it at anytime!" I disagreed contentedly, "Come on brother, you're just a little paranoid." I went on out back to finish the number.

One hot summer afternoon, J.P. came walking into the club with a shit-eating grin on his face from scoring with some chick he had earlier left with. She was hanging at the bar for sometime now, so I guess he was the first to dip his wick into her. "Parco, she wants to get it on with you! Ha, Ha, Ha," he hinted. "She's right around the corner man!" and he gave me her address. I took the hint, off and running I went. I was in the sack with her in a flash.

Days passed. J.P. came walking into the club with a serious look on his face, telling me that he got syphilis from the bitch. He told me I ought to go get checked. I took his advice and went to the clinic. I had to return in a week for results. I figured, what the fuck, since I probably have it already, I might as well go for another piece of ass from her. When I got the results from the hospital it was negative. No disease. Off I went to Cape Cod to my relatives place for a vacation. Sure enough, while I was there, my dick started burning and dripping yellow scum. I caught syphilis from the sloppy seconds I received. When I arrived back in Lawrence, I explained the situation to the brothers. Right away, they came through with a half-dozen bottles of penicillin. I gobbled them down like crossroads. The miracle worked. No more syphilis. That was some close call. We were through with that bitch.

The Calumet Club was always rolling from start to finish. One night, the Lawrence Detectives came barging in with high powered rifles stating that the bar would have to close due to the fact that they got a tip that the Angels were on their way down to demolish our club. I immediately went to the phone to give one of the Lowell members—Dirty Dave—a call. It was close to eleven p.m., and Dave answered. When I told him the bullshit he laughed, and told me to tell the cops to go sleep on it. He was going to bed. We had to go along with the cops, naturally, to shut down early. It was just another day in the night.

On the hot summer afternoons, the bar served its purpose. I was running from here to there, picking up babes, stopping for a couple of cold ones, and at the same time, my drug intake started to increase rapidly. One of the off-duty

Lawrence cops waved me over to his car. I got in and we went for a ride. He gave me a bullshit line that I tried to rape his so-called wife. I just listened, I guess he was looking for some money cause it would never have stuck, he probably figured I'd get paranoid or something and would come through. Instead, I let it in one ear and out the other. What are cops for anyway? Too fuck with your head? He never contacted me after that confrontation.

Life in General

There is only one way to make up your mind
Some beer and a lot of scotch 'til your thoughts are blind
Then you realize at the end, "wow is that me"
All the time you didn't know who the hell to be
A party and a party there, but your not really straight yet
To where you can place your path and not feel like a rat
An animal such as a deer always stays on the move
And I should hope that you can get into that groove
With no routine, it's the only way
And that means that you don't have to pray
Just hug the earth and keep on dreaming
Both at the same time and you will find a meeting
To live a life with super good health
Lots of friends and plenty of wealth

6

The Biker Runs

The Blessing of the Bikes was always a decent trip to follow-up on. It was a couple of weeks before the Laconia Run. After the bikes were blessed, there would be some partying or an event to follow up on for the remainder of the day. We would ride up in front of The Shrine of Our Lady, where priests would be, blessing our bikes as we rolled by the shrine with some holy water. After getting blessed, you would have to wait in line to head back down the hill with hundreds of bikers in front of you, to get back down to the public. I decided to take a short-cut by going downhill by the grass and I accidentally slid on the surface, landing on my ass. We would gather up to get to party at the hill climb event about 20 miles away, right over the border of Vermont. Everybody was partying their brains out. We would sit back and relax and watch the dirt bikers' race up a steep hill, to see who would first reach the destination. It was worth watching. Most of the bikes would flip over the rider's head before reaching the top. The hill was as close to a straight line from three quarters up. I didn't see one rider make it to the top, but it was sight to see.

All the bikers were getting tanked up on some booze or drug to lay back and mellow out on. We decided to start our own race on the flat-land to get a little action in on the ground. After watching a few runs, I decided to get up and perform my own little bit on the strip. I started racing an old friend from the Pallbearer's M.C. who was racing on a dirt bike. He was a former outlaw biker from the sixties. During the first run, he got the best of me. But once I got the feel of the track, I blue him away in the dust. I'd race one of the brothers, Fabian, and leave him right from the starting line. His rear wheel would be spinning in the dirt. Another brother would be getting on the track and we'd be off and running. There was a hump on the track that would put me in mid-air, banging second gear at the same time, coming back down on the winner's side of the track. I'd go for another run, and missing second gear, it was time for me to get off the track and watch the other brothers battle it out. Everything seemed to be going fine.

Everyone was having a great time, getting half gassed in the middle of the afternoon. Dude and Geronimo completed a few runs down the strip. As they decided to call it quits, a few outsiders wanted to test their skills and got on the starting line to go for a run at it. The problem was whoever called the start of the race didn't realize that Dude was coming back down the strip, and that it was too soon to start the race. BANG! One of the bikers collided with Dude. There was no way out of it. There was a van parked on the side where they collided. Neither one could avoid contact. Luckily, Dude got the least of the accident with just a few scrapes. The other biker went flying in mid-air, as if he was doing a front snap kick off the seat of his machine. An ambulance was called. He was in serious condition. We heard through the grapevine that he never made it through the crash.

The Laconia run of '74 was one hell of a weekend. I brought my ol'lady Cheryl with me. It was late Friday afternoon and the rain was starting to let up. We came fully prepared with the step van, a huge tent, sleeping bags, booze, drugs, and three ounces of high grade weed. On the way up, most of us were already stoned on some THC, speed, or a combination of both. When we got on the main drag, the showers let up, the sun started beaming through, and there was a rainbow. We found a spot to set camp and the party started. By nightfall, I was horny as a dog. I grabbed my sleeping bag, along with my ol'lady, and decided to move away from the crowd to get a piece of ass. After we got through, we just mellowed out for a bit. A bunch of bikers from Lawrence, who camped aside of us, were walking to our camp to join the party. They almost walked over us, not being able to see us under the sleeping bag. They laughed when I stuck my head out from under, since we were all very close friends, "Hey Parco," as they headed to party with my club. After we got through with our loving bit, we went back to the site to party it up.

Everyone was half lit by midnight. The next thing you know, some bikers were riding at full throttle. It was a sound to hear and a sight to see. It was one hell of a trip, you'd hear a couple of scoots dragging it out, then you'd hear sirens and see flashing lights chasing them down the road. This went on close to a few hours before dawn. It turned out to be a real show. I don't think that one of them got busted. They were always way ahead of the cruisers. I partied right into day break. Two dudes that hung with the club, Mark, a Vietnam Vet, and Brother, a space cadet, were playing head games with each other. One was drunk, the other was stoned out, walking in circles, mumbling nonsense, 'til they both decided to clash. They both were willing to get it on. While Mark used some of his martial arts techniques, Brother really got his ass kicked. He wound up with a dislocated shoulder that I know. That was the fireworks for the beginning of the day. I mean, what more could you ask for in less than a day? After the fight, some of the bikers started some more power runs, roaring down the strip, racing on the edge. It was some fuckin' sight to see.

The sun broke through the clouds by noon. The freeway was packed with bikers, some just rolling in. I got off just watching the whole scene. Jumpin Jack came by in the back of a pick-up truck and yelled out jokingly to me, "Parco, Linda wants to give you some head!" I was pretty well lit by then. It was one hell of an afternoon between all the drugs I ingested and my ol'lady. She and I decided to mellow out for a bit for a fresh start for the evening scene. While we were in the sack, *Easyriders* magazine came by and took a photo of our set-up for their Laconia issue. As we got up for the remaining afternoon, it was like refueling or getting tanked up for the rest of the weekend. By nightfall, my mind was in the *cosmos*. I was floating like an eagle in the sky. Preacher was really cooked. He decided to pull a nutty by going out in the breakdown lane, dropping his pants, and sitting on his helmet. He yelled out what helmets were only good for—to take a shit in. That was that. He started an argument with the bikers across the freeway from us. Before it amounted to anything, the cops showed up and grabbed him for protective custody. We were able to get him out of jail in a few hours. The vibes were floating so strongly, paranoia started creeping in. I noticed some strange character walking around our site in plain clothes. He was in and out of our tent. I thought he was an undercover agent. Finally, he split. It was some night, we were all partying our brains out.

When Sunday came, my mind was in another universe. Every biker seemed pretty well satisfied as to how the weekend turned out. On our way back through New Hampshire, we stopped at a lake to take a break and smoke a few numbers of the remaining herb. It was a beautiful afternoon. My ol'lady and I were waiting to get back to Lawrence to get it on again and my brother Ronnie invited us up to his pad to mellow out. He had one of his gals with him so you know where he was heading, the bedroom. We took the living room couch. As we were getting it on, I got the strangest vibes. I felt that Ronnie wanted to have a swap meet, swapping babes. It was more than vibes, it was voices. I heard Ronnie's voice, along with my ol'lady's, without words being spoken. It was all inside my head, like telepathic, almost real, maybe it was real. I didn't question it. I guess I was over-amplifying from all the drugs I consumed over the weekend. Nothing went any further than my vivid imagination.

My ol'lady had such a tight pussy I'd get my rocks off faster then a wild rabbit. She was cherry when we first met. After the day went through, I was able to crash finally. The next day I was able to wake up with my head on my shoulders, back to earth level, back to myself again. It was one hell of a bizarre weekend I'll never forget.

What I know through my studies of the occult, nothing is an accident, such as cause and effect, synchronism, the paranormal. Nothing is predestined, unless hidden within the gods. There are obstacles we have to face. Shit happens. It isn't a perfect world. We're here to improve ourselves and others despite it all. So you can change your path in life when you want to or find your path. *Evil* spelled backwards is *live*, and a lot of living I've done so far.

We decided to make a serious run up to Three Rivers, Canada for a week. We had a pick-up truck that one of the prospects drove up in case of any breakdown. Zap was a hang-around, so we invited him along for the trip. It started raining the minute we left Massachusetts. He stayed in the back of the pickup all the way up, since we had a couple other passengers up front. We had other runs that we encountered in the rain, but this was the longest. We got drenched all the way up to the Canadian Border. While we were crossing, I had to take a wicked piss. I asked the guard where to find the outhouse and joking, he asked if I had any drugs to get rid of. He pointed to the rest area to the right. A few of the bros also had to drain their kidneys. It was cool and raw. My jeans were still wet, but we already had plans to party with the Gitans M.C. We were going to connect with them at one of their hang-around bars. Everything rolled in progression. The bar was loaded with free shots of whiskey, and without hesitation, LSD was distributed pretty quickly. By the time the whiskey warmed me, I was starting to get off on the acid. A little weed to lighten up the subject, and off and running was the night. Wilkie and I decided to see the city in 3-D as the other brothers went to party over their clubhouse. What a fuckin' trip we were having, first time seeing the city, cars flashing by in the night life, city lights blaring. We spent a few hours just strolling along like we were part of the city. We eventually grabbed a cab back to the clubhouse. When we got back, everyone was in a mellow state of mind. Within a few hours we were off and running to the big city.

It was Three Rivers, to get a motel for a week. The Gitans escorted us out of city. They were at war with the Popeye M.C., so they rode with us up the main drag and wished us a good trip for the rest of the run. When we got to the city, we rented a couple of double bunks at one of the motels. We had some women with us, one, soon to become a club Mama.

It turned out to be a non-stop party. THC was the most common taste around the city. There were some heavy underground clubs to party in. We had some wild times. When we got associated with Popeye, it was a non-stop high from then on. They had a dynamite clubhouse to party in, with nothing surrounding them except railroad tracks and vacant turf. They knew before we arrived that we had already partied with the Gitans, but they didn't hold anything against us, since we didn't know what the score was 'til we got there.

Butchie and Dude showed up a couple of days later, after we left for the run. They both had to take care of some business prior to leaving. Dude was one crazy fucker. When he pulled up on his machine, he almost ran into one of the Popeye members. While we were at their clubhouse, we all got turned on to some pure THC. They had a blasting bonfire in the backyard, and inside, a bar, pool table, and bedrooms. One Popeye member came into the pool room with a loaded single pump shotgun, asking jokingly what he should shoot. Dude, playing pool, told him "shoot the eight ball in the corner pocket, *Ha-Ha-Ha-Ha-Ha*!" He was always joking around. I decided to get on my Harley and take a ride into the city. I was passing a bar with a few bikes parked out front, so I decided to stop and have a couple. I got to talking to the bikers. They were from the U.S. We had a few drinks and decided to go outside and talk some more before splitting. There was a mini-bike parked aside of us. One of the bikers started horsing around by picking it up. He tried to hook it on to his sissy-bar. We decided to split. We were all heading back to the Popeye clubhouse. We wound up splitting in different directions, power-shifting through the first intersection. I got lost in the city and during my power-shifting, I blew my headlight. As I was passing some Canadian Police they were staring at me in awe, as I asked them which way back to the clubhouse. He said "*Left, Left.*" Somehow I made it back with the luck of pure instinct. Snake was just ready to take a ride in search of me. He figured something went wrong, and was ready to try to track me down. The other bikers that I was drinking with laughed over the whole ordeal. We were all fucked up anyway in the process of having a decent, good time.

It was time to make it back to the motel and party a bit. I was so stoned I couldn't even get it up to score with the Mama we brought along. Other than that, the other bros all had a good time just partying, or scoring with their ol'ladies. The night went by like it always seemed to do, fast and easy.

By the end of the week, we all packed up, checked for minor adjustments on the bikes, and decided to take the country road through Vermont. We stopped to smoke some weed that Butchie stashed before he crossed the border on the way up. He usually would stash it in his handle bars, but he didn't take any chance crossing the border. We all got a good buzz on, the country roads in Vermont were like life in the old years. The tune came in my mind.

Signs Signs

Everywhere there's signs
Blocking up the scenery
Breaking up my mind
Do this, don't do that
Can't you read the sign

The country roads were true nature. No signs, no signals, just nature. It was freedom all the way home. When we hit New Hampshire, we cruised home with a breeze. When we made it back home, we were still ready to roll. So to mellow out we decided to go get a bite to eat and shoot the shit for a little while before we all went our way to go and crashed for the night.

7

Road Captain Goes Vice President

After the closing of the Calumet Club, we were in luck of having our own 24-7 clubhouse at our convenience. We were able to handle the rent money through our club dues, along with the outsiders that showed up at all strange hours to the early dawning hours. The early seventies was the real peak of the drug industry, Speed, LSD, THC, Downs and Weed. It was all available, along with the women, and naturally, motorcycles filled the void, so to speak. It was like an imaginary green pasture we were living in. Anything we wanted, we got it.

Snake, along with one of his prospects, built the entire bar. Like the real thing, the walls were painted black. A long black-light was positioned above, mounted right below the ceiling. The house was rocking, the house was rocking. Snake and I practically lived there. The parties were non-stop. The brothers were popping in and out, along with the female gender. It all started in *the void*, which is emptiness. It was like a warped, time frame. It was *too much, too little, too late*. I'd be getting fucked in the afternoon, she'd leave and I would get a few zzzzz's. I'd wake up, back down the stairs, another babe would be sitting on the stairway, grab her hand, then back upstairs in the sack. Laid and par-laid, as the saying goes, and I loved it. Nancy was one of my on and off ol'ladies. She was connected with a group of chicks from the suburbs, who called themselves the sweat-hogs. Boy, were they spaced. I'd be fucking more than one gal from the group, while Butch would be fucking another. During that time of the month as in women's problem, Nancy would have a script of percodans. We'd be at the clubhouse laid-back, getting off to 4 or 5 pills at a time, 'til a cold sweat would be rolling off me, along with the chills to follow. I felt like a cold turkey case. She'd grab me by the hand and take me for a walk around the block to get my motor running once again. She was something else. I did have a lot of loving with her. She was some space cadet.

When Jack and Zap returned back from the west coast, they traveled through Florida picking up a couple of chicks on the way. Heading up north they made some friends in Georgia, which eventually traveled up to visit us at our club house. Zap made one of the gals his ol'lady, while the other, hung around the house for some time, having fun with the bros. I'd be working on my bike after being up all night, just mellowing out. After cranking for 48 hours, the beers would bring me down, one step at a time. Before noon, one of the gals would be grilling some Cheese Whiz sandwiches. It was great on a hot summer morning, passing them down through the window to me. It would make the start of the day blossom just right. By noon the club would start rolling. The music would get turned up, the partying would just happen. J.P. would be hugging and kissing one of the hang-around babes, just as his ol'lady would be pulling up to the club-house. It was a sight to see. She would yell at him through the car window and he would come out of the house and into the car with her, and they would settle the differences between them.

As I was riding through the neighborhood, I ran into some redneck southerner who was building an eighty-inch Flathead. We got associated with each other. I introduced him to Fuck-Up and Zap. Zap was still prospecting. He was getting into some dirty business just to make ends meet. The next thing I know, Zap comes walking into the clubhouse with just a little help from the bros with the 80" Flathead in pieces. Fuck-Up made a deal with him on the motor. The rest of the parts were already distributed to the right people. A few days later, the owner retaliated and blasted a shotgun shell through one of our windows. There was only one prospect in the house. Luckily no one got hit. We could read between the lines. The next day I did enough crank to choke a horse. I brought Zap with me to visit the southerner. When you're speeding your word *is your word* so I was able to throw a good bullshit line. "One of the pellets from the blast hit one of our gal's eye and one of us noticed your car passing by, so if anything happens to her, you're going to regret it." He just listened in astonishment. What I drilled into his head, he digested. After we left him, we knew he wouldn't fuck with us anymore.

We had a former junkie friend named J.C., who Dude first brought into the club as a hang-around. We gave him a room to crash in and he had high hopes of becoming a prospect. The brothers used to work out together. A lot of sparring, kick boxing. You name it. We would go around trying to catch each other off guard. Who would be quick enough to out-wit the other? This way, we would attempt to be alert all the time for the real scuffle. Somehow, J.C. became a punching bag. Dude set him up to take a few blows. He never made it to become a member and after a while we had to tell him to take a hike. If you didn't have a bike, you'd be lucky to be a hang-around. If we were sure you were going to get a machine on the road, we would consider you a prospect.

After 2 a.m., a lot of the late night bikers would come over to the house to party for a few hours. Some close friends would distribute a few lines of coke, and we'd party for a few more hours past dawn. The house was always rocking, whether it was fucking, or getting stoned, working on the scoot in between times, or deciding on going on a stiff drunk for a day or two, the club members couldn't complain about hardly anything at the meetings.

When election time came about, Snake got voted out as president. Butchie got the vote in, and I became vice president, leaving my road captain position behind. The house threw a birthday party for me. At the same time, we had a going away party for Dude, since he got convicted on a stabbing beef that he got sentenced for 6 months in the Plymouth House of Correction. It seemed to me as a non-stop party. I never even made it out of the recliner chair. A good friend of mine, Gino came by and gave me a nude poster to hang on my bedroom wall. Other friends had some sort of gift to hand to me. The beef Dude had turned out to be a self defense rap, but it didn't go that way in court. Luckily, his father was a judge, or else he could have got some serious time out of the deal, since he was a convicted felon already. His father also got him in one of the best jails in the state, but, time is time, don't matter which way you look at it. Dude, who was close to 6 feet tall and about 200 pounds, was so pissed off he almost started a fight with my buddy Gino, who was about 6 foot 2 and about 250 pounds to boot. Over what, I think it was just a shoulder to shoulder nudge. Dude was so bull shit you could see the fire from within him, burning just to let off a little steam at any given moment. He was at his peak, ready to fuck with anyone. He went through a lot of shit in the past, including being active in the Navy in the 60's during the Vietnam era. Luckily, he cooled down, and attended to his ol'lady and the party went on for the rest of night. I was on LSD with plenty of brew that kept me in duration of that recliner for the entire evening.

One afternoon, Jumpin Jack came through with some peanut butter methamphetamine. The stuff got me so high, voices inside my head started to amplify. I guess I consumed too much all at once. Snake had some dynamite weed and I believe that only made my mind accelerate. I could here the birds chirping as if they were talking to me. "Clean your tubes clean your tubes," was what I was hearing while the birds chirped. I never heard such a statement from a human source, never mind read of it, but I knew exactly what it meant—an orgasm. The Paranormal through the Cosmos was moving in with the call of nature-known as the Second Attention. "Living an ordinary life in a non-ordinary way," it was time to come back to the First Attention. I have studied all of this information through the book "The teachings of Don Juan: a Yaqui way of knowledge" by Carlos Castaneda and his continuous book publishing on sorcery. He put over a dozen books out on the subject. This was all in focus within a twenty-four hour span. It was time to get some fire water to sort of cool my jets. I started to feel as if I was coming back down to surface level at that. I decided to go up to Lowell to party with some Angels at their hang-around bar, Nick's Bar. I brought my prospect along, Zap, to break him in a little better. When we got there, Suave Dave asked me for a ride. He had a deal in progress. We took a quick run, but no deal went through.

We went back to the bar. I was feeling mellow as the drinks went down. As the closing of the bar came, I was in the right frame of mind to tie a good night on. I asked Hawkeye if he wanted to join us. He grabbed his ol'lady and we headed back to Lawrence. When we got back to Zap's apartment, I sent him over to Jack's place to pick up some more of that speed. Everything went through. Hawkeye and I were up to dawn, rapping about politics, and a wide range of subjects. We finally got a little shut eye after talking ourselves to sleep.

When we awoke, we complemented each other for having such a good rap session overnight. His ol'lady slept through the whole ordeal. We took a ride up to New Hampshire to check out a few junk yards for a master cylinder for an old pick-up truck Hawkeye owned. He lucked out. Off and rolling we went, back to Lowell to Hook's apartment. I was pretty crispy after speeding for a couple of days. Hawkeye noticed it and asked me "You got it-okay?" I nodded yes.

No wonder why they call him Hook. He had a whole collection of meat and ice hooks neatly hanging on his wall. Zap was amazed himself. We stuck around for a bit, smokin' a number, and shooting the breeze, as they would say. We planned to meet that evening back at Nick's Bar to have a few together. I was thinking of becoming a Hell's Angel. It was crossing my mind. Hawkeye and I were talking about an idle Harley that I knew of that could become a five finger discount. I sat down with Fuck-Up and we started talking about the details I needed to know of joining the club. That night at Nick's, everything seemed to go synchronistically. He told me specifically that I'd have to go through a mud-check, which is fighting another member. Other than that, everything seemed fine. After I finished a beer, I got up to go to the head. On the way, Hawkeye hinted to me about that bike, "When are you getting me that Harley?" I joked back, "Yeah, Fuck-you." I was too much in a hurry to hit the head. When I came from the head, I sat back with Fuck-Up. Hook came storming over, telling me to get up. As I stood, he asked me what I had said to Hawkeye. "Fuck-you!" I said. "What did you say to him?" he repeated. "Fuck-you!" I knew that it was curtains. The next thing that happened was a round house of hooks that flattened me in seconds. "Get up, Mutha-Fucker, Get up!" he said scornfully. I got up and stood face-to-face with him. Man, what a tough bastard he was. No wonder he was president at that time and why his name was Hook. He put his arm over my shoulder and walked me to the bar, bought us a couple of shots of whiskey with a few beer chasers. He pointed to Zap at the end of the bar and told the bar tender to give him a glass of milk. He looked at Zap and yelled to him "And Drink It!" Zap didn't say a word, and did what he was told. Hook turned back to me. We both downed the booze, "You know what's happening?" He basically was meaning the mud-check. "You know what you're up against?" He meant the initiation is all or nothing, no fucking around. "Yeah," I answered, we killed the chasers while we were breaking bread. We separated and went back to where we were at, like nothing ever happened.

The night went on with more booze intake while Hawkeye decided to pull a fast one on me. He called me to the other side of the bar. Next thing you know he stated, "Say Fuck-You to Me, Mutha-Fucker?" He suckered me with a fast one, right in the face. Without any thought, I slammed him right in the nose, splitting it to bleed, kicked him right in the balls. Fuck-Up came after me from the back. I turned and gave him a back-kick in the gut. At the same time I was getting prepared for Hawkeye, but he was ahead of me with a set of nunchakus sticks. *Whack*! It hit me right on top of my head. *"Kick me in the balls, you mutha-fucker?"* I fell right to the floor. The impact was so intense the fire-works went off in my head. Fuck-Up started a hassle with Zap. They ended up in a push and tug type wrestling match. I headed to the bathroom to wash all the blood off my face. As I was walking back toward the bar, three Lowell cops were standing with Hook, Hawkeye, and Fuck-Up, trying to get a low down on what the fuck happened. The cops asked me if I was in a fight. I told them that I just fell on the floor. I kept on walking, heading toward the front door. One of the cops followed me, grabbed me from behind, threw me on one of the bar tables, and gave me a round house of punches. What a fuckin' night. Three strikes! You're out! Out the door and into the car we went.

When we got back to Lawrence, Zap and his ol'lady advised me to go to the hospital. When I got there, the doctor asked me what happened. I had two black eyes, a broken nose, and I needed stitches on top of my head. I told him that I had a flat tire and while I was changing it, some hoodlums decided to roll me. They took the tire iron from me and hit me in the head. "You're lucky you're alive!" the doctor quoted. All in all, I hardly felt any pain. I believe it was from all the injuries I sustained from the past. They just seemed to make me more tolerable and strong head wise.

8

Prelude to Disaster

A couple of weeks after the Lowell mayhem, we were throwing a Halloween party with the Angels invited. It was being held at Jack's property. It was all pre-planned. We had marijuana in the tomato sauce for the spaghetti, along with THC in the punch. There was a live band performing. Both floors of the building were open for the party. Peter on the first floor had a light show going with some Pink Floyd music playing. If you wanted to mellow out, that was the place to be—black lights shining on florescent posters. There were over two hundred people peacefully partying. The Lawrence Police arrived to check out the scene. They must of heard the loud music playing while they were cruising by. Everything looked fine. They couldn't notice anything going out of hand. There was no dope being smoked, it was in the sauce. Jumpin Jack came out with the assumption that he was keeping the trouble off the streets by having the party. The Hell's Angels haven't even arrived yet and the cops were baffled over the whole ordeal. The next thing you know, Jack yelled out a long *Heeee-Haaa*. Then everyone joined in, *"Heeeeee-Haaaaaa."* One cop looked at the other with the attitude that they should split. Everyone laughed and cheered!

The Hell's Angels finally arrived on their Harleys. It was a sight to see, all the bikes lined up in front of the building. One of their prospects, Harpy, was the first to make it upstairs. Some wise ass started mouthing off, saying to Harpy that he was connected with the Devil's Disciples M.C. He didn't realize how many Angels were on their way upstairs to the party. He told Harpy he should split, just as Suave Dave and a couple of other Angels walked in. Dave cold-cocked him and ripped his shirt off his shoulder saying "Show me your Devil's Disciples tattoo, Mutha-Fucker!" The dude laid low. Miles, Jack's hip father-in-law, thought it was going to turn out to be a bad night and asked me what I was going to do about this. I didn't say anything, while Hawkeye gave me that rare Hawkeye wink. The dude had it coming to him.

Dave, Harpy, and I decided to go back outside to see what was happening. Tom-Tom was crossing the street while a car cut in front of him. Tom backed off to the driver's window and gave the driver an upper-cut slam right to the head. We walked around the block to see if there were any dicks parked on the street. Sure enough, they were sitting there. We just kept on walking. The cops formed a Riot Squad one street over from the party. We went back upstairs to join the party and enjoy the band. It was about one in the morning when the Angels decided to split. Most of our brothers had other places to go. I had to get one of my lady friend's home. We were off and rolling. That was when the Riot Squad decided to raid the party. Snake was the only brother they pulled in for protective custody. There was a few other party animals that they decided to pop. Altogether, it was a decent night for a party to take place.

As it seems, newspaper journalists never get the story exactly correct. The Angels never had a chapter in Reading. I just want to make that clear. Here is the low down from the article that got printed.

RIOT SQUAD ENDS PARTY Nov. 1, 1974

Lawrence police called out the riot squad on Halloween night to break up a "large, drunken party" at Newton and Rowe Streets.

Police said the crowd, which swelled to 300 at one point, included the Reading chapter of "the famous Hell's Angels gang."

Five men were taken into protective custody and another, John Oliver, 23, of North Reading, was arrested and charged with possession of marijuana.

Otherwise, the party was broken up without incident.

Police said this morning they had heard complaints about the party all night from South Lawrence residents.

They said there were up to 300 people partying in the streets and Hell's Angels' motorcycles were jammed in everywhere.

About 12:30 a.m., police decided to break up the party.

Men from the early night shift were held over to join forces with the late night men, and extra men were called in from Methuen, Andover and North Andover.

Together the made up a riot squad of more than 50 men, all equipped with riot helmets and night sticks.

As the men formed a line on Crosby Street, near the scene of the party, two men were dispatched in a cruiser to Newton and Rowe to warn the crowd that the party was over.

There were still about 100 people in the streets at the time, about 1:30 a.m., police said. They were told over the bullhorn they had 10 minutes to clear out on their own. "Go and get your army," someone shouted at the two men in the cruiser.

Despite the challenge, the party had broken up on its own when police returned after 10 minutes.

Five men still on the scene were drunk and violent so they were held over night in protective custody but were not arrested.

They were to be released this morning once they were sober.

Aside from the big party at Newton and Rowe, Halloween night was generally quiet in Greater Lawrence.

"Reprinted courtesy of The Salem News"

9

"He's Got a Knife"

A week or so after the Halloween bash, we got invited to a party in Reading, where Jack was originally from, and where most of the former party crowd came from. The same band was going to be playing there too, so it sounded like a good night out. I was over Butchie's pad, getting a good buzz on some crank. It was a crisp autumn night. We were listening to the radio, when the astrologer came on with a reading for the evening. He stated that it was a good night for a buzz, but not for any social gatherings. I'll never forget that reading, since it turned to be one hell of a night, and I mean one hell of a night. Butch decided on some other plans, so I went over to Zap's apartment and have him give me a tattoo before we left for the party. We met at Jack's. There was Tonto, Preacher, and a couple of ol'ladies. Peter came along, since he was more or less a hang-around with the club. We picked up a couple of cases of beer so we wouldn't walk in empty handed.

Captain Video was already at the party since he lived the next town over. I was in the right frame of mind to sit down and enjoy the beer and the band. The music was playing fine and my mind was picking up just good vibes. Tonto and Preacher were already burnt out on something they were goofing on, so they decided to relax outside of the party. There were maybe twenty to thirty people, nothing like our bash, but it felt good with a lesser crowd, then standing room only. I decided to get up and grab me another beer. At the same time, I bounced into Zap. He was in a conversation with some Reading chumps. I got some bad vibes the first second. "What's happening?" I asked. Before he could answer, one of the Reading chumps turned to me and said, "I'll tell you what's happening, Fuck-you! Fuck-you!" They were arguing over whose beer was whose. While I caught the drift, I thought it was some fuckin' crazy reason to start a fight over. The next thing I knew he landed a sucker punch on me. I got shoved against the wall, knocked down to the floor, and then kicked in the head. I landed on some empty beer bottles that got broken with my elbow, which a piece of the glass lodged in. That did it, I decided to open my buck knife and stand up to defend myself. Just as I was standing, some dude came at me with a full swing, he got the blade right in his gut, and down for the count. It was automatic reflex. There was not enough time for a single thought. I was swaying from left to right with the blade in front of me to keep anyone from retaliating. They finally tried to overpower me by grabbing hold of my wrist and hand holding the knife. The hand and the blade supernaturally became one like they were welded together. Maybe the speed helped, I don't know. They couldn't pry my fingers open to let go of it. *"Let go of him, he will put the knife away!"* The women yelled. I was finally able to break away from them. How I did it was a miracle. I thought, "If I give in, I'll be a goner."

The fight wasn't over yet. They had Zap in the other room breaking beer bottles over his head, and beating the shit out of him. Tonto just walked in, wondering what the fuck was going on. He caught on quick. We barreled our way into the other room. Jack was trying to get everyone off of Zap, *"He's got a knife! He's got a knife!"* Everyone was yelling. I rushed in towards Zap with the blade in my hand, everyone broke loose off him. We gathered together and made a quick decision to split. As I was walking out of the basement door—*Whack!* I got hit with a baseball bat above my right eye, splitting my eyebrow. Stars and stripes floated over my head. I headed to the nearest tree to get my balance. Blood was pouring from the cut. Preacher was lying down close by. He came to the minute he heard all the commotion. "What's going on man? What's going on?" He jumped up in a flash. "Take out your knife, Take out your knife!" I told him in dismay. Preacher went searching for anyone that looked felonious, but the assailants split. Jack's ol'lady came over to me with a towel packed with ice. We headed to the car we drove up in.

The cops arrived and came walking towards our vehicle before we could split. I put the ice-pack to my lap so I wouldn't be noticed. They asked Peter for his license and registration. He had his license, but no registration. They said that they were looking for someone with a knife. Peter told them that he had to get ME to the hospital. The cops didn't hold us. Everyone said I needed stitches. I was reluctant. We finally made it on the road and off to the hospital.

While we were at the hospital, we were running around like chickens that just had their heads cut off. We were just going "Big Time" at this type of shit. For all I knew, I could have caused serious damage to the dude I stuck. I didn't want to go to the emergency in the first place, but everyone told me that my eyebrow needed stitches or it would never heal right. I didn't even have them check the cut on my elbow and only found out years later that the glass that cut it had imbedded in it. I just wanted out. Zap had to get treated too. He had so many cuts from the bottles they slammed him with.

The next morning, Zap and I went over to the apartment of one of his girlfriends, which we left as our address at the hospital. Fuck-Up was there. The minute we came inside, he told us that the heat was by, and I was in some serious shit. I asked Judy for some alcohol so I could clean my blade. Fuck-Up came onto me with a comment, "My birthday's coming up soon and I sure could use a blade!" I just ignored him while he got back into flirting with Judy. The dicks had walked off with a grass plant Zap had growing there.

I was going mad. Schizophrenia was creeping in on me. The newspaper put the story out that two Evil Spirits were wanted for a stabbing at a party in Reading. I was driving a '65 Ford Galaxy. The frame was cracked and it rolled like an accordion. The radio would tune in and out of stations, and in between, it would make its own sound with some strange vibrations, like it was trying to give me some messages. Paranoia set in, whenever I saw a cruiser. I felt that they were specifically looking for me. Maybe so, I didn't know what to expect next. My car stalled. I couldn't get it started. I called Jack, but his wife answered the phone and told me she didn't know where he was at. She'd let him know the situation I was in once he made it back. I finally got the car running, and headed directly to Jack's apartment. The Captain was there. We sat down together and lit up a bowl and crushed THC with some high grade grass to burn it with. That was one of Video's habits to start a conversation. He went on and on, about how corruption was tied with the government and the corporations. Jack arrived. He was already on cloud nine. He was planning to split with Zap to the west coast, since he already had some warrants out on him. Zap was wanted on the same charges that I was facing. By the time I decided to split, I was floating from that smoke. While I was driving my car, I felt like I was going through "The Electric Kool-Aid Acid Test." The newspaper screwed up the whole story, saying the stabbing was connected with some fight involving the Hell's Angels and the Evil Spirits. It mentioned the Halloween party we had in Lawrence. I was on the run for a couple of weeks before I decided to turn myself in. One of the detectives that knew me fairly well asked, "Hey Parco, what are you doing coming in without your colors on?" I didn't give him any answer. The marijuana plant they picked up while looking for me was sitting on his desk wilting. "The Reading police have a warrant for you. You're being charged with Assault with Intent to Murder, Assault with a Dangerous Weapon." We just stared at each other. "I'm going to radio to them in, they will be down to pick you up!"

Once I arrived at the Reading station, the dicks started questioning me with the look that they were going to rough me up to get their answers. I just hung tough and didn't give them the right time of day. Everything went along in the legal procedure. The next morning on arraignment, I was sent to the Billerica House of Correction on $500 cash bail. My brother Butch came up with the cash to have my sister bail me out later that afternoon. The funny thing about Butch was that I offered him my scoot in turn for an airfare to the west coast with the Flash and Zap to dodge the rap, he wouldn't come through, but when the bail was set, he was right on top of it.

I was a free man finally. I didn't have to run from the law, but had to carry the burden on my shoulder on facing the court trial. My witnesses assembled with my attorney and me. My attorney was Captain Video's brother-in-law. We said everything as it happened. We just left out the part that I used my knife to end the disruption. This guy was really sharp and he knew what he was doing. When we went to District Court, we went in front of a one-armed judge who was fairly lenient. He threw out the intent to murder charge, and bounded the assault with a dangerous weapon over to a grand jury on probable cause. When my lawyer and I talked confidentially, he told me that he could tell that the victim and his witnesses were lying. He still questioned my validity as to whether I did the stabbing or not. I said it wasn't me. He mentioned if I wanted him to defend me for grand jury, it would cost me $3000. I couldn't come up with that type of money, so I lost a good defense lawyer. I really didn't worry that much over the situation, even though it could end up with a maximum of a ten year stretch. I tried keeping my cool. The waiting was the hardest part, and what a long strange trip it turned out to be. Here is the newspaper article that was printed. The writer didn't get the correct story.

MAN IS STABBED AT PARTY Nov.9, 1974

Two members of the Evil Spirits, a Lawrence-Methuen motorcycle gang are suspects in a stabbing last night in Reading.

Fred Verville, 23, 25 Holly Road, Reading, was admitted to Melrose-Wakefield Hospital last night after he was stabbed in the stomach at a house party on Haverhill Street in Reading.

The hospital refused to release any information on Verville's condition this morning, but one spokesman said Verville had not been admitted to the intensive care unit, indicating his condition was not critical.

Reading police said this morning they were searching for two members of the motorcycle gang in connection with the stabbing. Police said the gang was based in the Lawrence-Methuen area.

Last week, on Halloween night, Lawrence police broke up a "loud, drunken party" in South Lawrence, dispersing a crowd they said included members of the Reading chapter of the Hell's Angels motorcycle gang.
Reading police said they were unaware of the incident, and were not investigating the possibility of a feud between the rival gangs.
"Reprinted courtesy of The Salem News"

10

The Waiting

The runs were fantastic there were always some place to travel to. Our regular place was a short distance away, Salisbury Beach. We would party at the Bowery Club, the Frolics, or right out on the beach-front. We had received word that two of the Lowell Hell's Angels that we knew very well, R.B. and Whiskey George, got snuffed down in Florida. We didn't get all the details until one of the members Mousey was passing by the Bowery. He saw us hanging out front and stopped to let us know that everything was being taken care of and we were welcomed to the wake up in Lowell. I attended the wake. There were more Angels then you could count. We got the full download of what actually happened. Shakey Al, also known as Oskie, ripped off the club and split to Florida and merged in with the Outlaws-another M.C. R.B. and Whiskey went down to take care of business. The Outlaws took advantage of them, shot them in the head, and sunk them in a quarry. It is said that Shakey got ousted along with them, but I heard different from a former Angel. Other than that, I'll let the story rest, as they rest in peace. Ever since then, it has been an all out war across the country between both rival clubs.

We had a friend that wanted to put his name on the voting ballot in the city of Lawrence for mayor. He was a former junkie, so he knew what the street problems actually were. He got interviewed by a small press newspaper called "*Today.*" He knew the editor, so he mentioned us to him, and he offered to do a cover story of us. This was the year 1975 and it turned to be the closing of the Vietnam War. It seemed to me later, that it was more or less, a domino effect year, where another would bite the dust, another would bite the dust, and on and on. When our picture showed up on the newspaper, the headlines were "*These chaps aren't affiliated with your Neighborhood Local Rotary Club, and they do shocking and frightening things!*" The headline was something to that nature, damn right, we were mutha-fuckin' crazy! We had a watchdog that was half Doberman, half shepherd, castrated and his name was Fenian. He was trained to attack while being chained. Let him loose, he would be your best friend. He used to enjoy being taking off the chain and I'd take him for a long walk or for the afternoon at that. I felt that we could communicate through telepathic thoughts, that was how burnt out I was most of the time. I thought if I ever considered doing a serious robbery, he would be my conspirator. Talk about being crispy, hearing voices in my head was a way of living from all the drugs I consumed in the process. Along with some serious whacks to the head that I accumulated, I was a perfect candidate for the position of vice president.

The '75 Laconia Run was the strangest weekend I ever encountered with the club. Just the planning for it started out negatively. The state outlawed roadside camping. Bad vibes were entering the entire nation since the Vietnam War had just ended. We had to get our own campsite in a private setting ahead of time. Preacher and I went up to make reservations ahead of time. One night in Loudon, on our way back, driving through a thick mountain fog, we got pulled over for a routine check, since we had Mass plates. They wrote us up for some dumb awful traffic violation like driving while blind through the night. We couldn't see ten feet in front of us. By the time we made it to Manchester, the fog lifted. We made it back to the clubhouse with few problems. When the weekend arrived, everyone was roused up to party, as usual. We were all half lit on some foreign substance by the time we got settled down to party. I don't know what Snake was on that night, but he just kept on staring at me in a negative way, like playing head games with him self. My mind was always rolling. Sometimes I'd lose it, but most of the time I'd be able to keep my head on my shoulders. One night I was tripping on some decent LSD over my brother's Ronnie's apartment, along with a cool hang-around friend named Heavy. The next thing while we were starting to peak, I was hearing Heavy's voice inside my head saying *"Cut the fuckin' shit and shut the fuck up! Cut the fuckin' shit and shut the fuck up!"* It went on over and over again. He was sitting right beside me on the couch and I'd look at him and notice that his lips weren't moving or his mouth wasn't opening. It surely was a strange trip. Sometimes I'd lose it for forty eight to seventy two hours, wonder how I'd make it back to ground level. I finally realized that everything counted, since I am an Aquarius, an air sign. They are born dreamers, communicators.

In any event, the party went on. We got buzzed and boozed up. That was it. Snake stared at me, looking for a fight. In return, I didn't consider it something too serious. What the hell, he was gunning for it. The bros said take it somewhere else, so we did, out into the woods. We were both persistent, heading away from the brothers, finding our spot. Only the light from the moon shined on us. We stopped, took our positions, stood and stared and off we went. It turned into a wrestling match. We tumbled and rolled on the ground. I got on top of him. My first instinct had me place my finger tips right on top of his eyeballs, just ready to tear his mutha-fuckin' eyeballs out. Snake started moaning for mercy. It brought my sub-conscious to let up on him. I would have blinded him, or even ripped one or both of his mutha-fuckin' eyeballs right out of the mutha-fuckin' Canuck skull of his. Was I right? Was I wrong? Fuckin' Snake took advantage of my let go. He flipped me over and punched my lights out. No mercy. He then got up and walked back to the brothers, leaving me with clouds in my head. I got up, turning around in the darkness. I was trying to figure which way back to the campsite. When I made it back to the brothers, the manager of the campsite walked me to the bathhouse with some clean towels to wash up with, since my nose was bleeding. The cold water cleaned everything up, I felt like myself again. What a fucked-up situation it turned out to be. The brothers took it for granted. Snake felt proud of himself for being the winner. I didn't say anything about the fight. It wouldn't have mattered anyway. All I know is if I carried out the fight without any conscience for him, he would have been permanently blinded out of at least one eye and I would have felt guilty over the whole ordeal. Who knows what the brothers would have thought of me if I fucked him up. Worse than what he already had from his previous accidents. Snake was still recovering from his last accident where he almost lost a foot. I guess it was all due to the drug intake and the wild life we have been living the past couple of years. We were both pretty well burnt to a bacon crisp. We just kept on partying over the weekend.

When we made it back to the clubhouse, most of the brothers went their separate ways. It was a long weekend and some of the bros had to be up for work in the morning. Just as a few of us made it to the house, Snake decided to pull a nutty on Butchie. Zap was right behind him. Snake used the excuse that Butchie was shooting too much speed, and needles were against the club rules. But mainly it was jealousy, since all the other brothers took care of their own business. Snake was the real member that was losing it. Other than that, he could have waited for a meeting to discuss the situation, man to man. Butchie's ol'lady was right behind him and broke a bottle over Snake's head. Butch decided to turn his colors in as president after that time.

A special election took place. Quick Nick got voted in president, and I was able to keep my position as vice president. Everything seemed to be working out fairly well. I was handling more pussy to keep me pretty much occupied, when time was at its least. If it wasn't this sweat hog or another mama we were banging from the past, it would be some new encounter. If I needed to keep filled in on one babe, I'd send my brother Tonto over to her place, to keep her pre-occupied while I'd be scoring with another past lover. It was just another way of life. Between the brothers and the fill of women, I was feeling my oats like a thoroughbred racer. Between Jumpin Jack, Zap, and I, along with a couple of mamas, we'd get an orgy going between fucking and sucking. If it wasn't that, we would have a righteous old sweat-hog that would ride the train to the last car-the caboose.

Heavy was an old friend and a regular hang-around with the club. He invited some of the brothers to the birthday party that his ol'lady was throwing for him. I decided to attend the gig. And man, did I get a quick buzz from all of the wine and the weed that was distributed. I decided to leave the party early. Some of the other brothers were up Salisbury Beach and they were expecting me to show up. The beach was one of our regular stomping grounds so to speak. I was riding up Interstate 495 when all of a sudden my bike started stalling out. I pulled over to the breakdown lane, noticed that I had run out of gas. Some vehicle stopped to see if they could help. They didn't have a gas container, but they were cool enough people to hand me a few bucks to cover the cost of the gas. That was nice of them. A second vehicle stopped by. A guy got out of the car. He had a gas container, and was willing to get me the gas out of his own pocket. He didn't want any cash. I lay back in the breakdown lane and started to nod out, when I noticed the headlights of the gas man pulling up behind me. Everything went cool refilling my tank.

So and off and running I went to join the party that was happening near the beach-side parking area. While riding up the strip, I decided to bang second gear and lifted the front wheel off the ground. Then I headed to park it for the evening. The State Police came walking over towards me, to tell me to slow it down a bit. I agreed without any problem, and they went on their merry go way. As I walked on the beach, Snake and J.P. were sitting back with a few other friends, blowing some weed that was strong enough to choke a horse. I decided to join in. The smoke helped me to sober up and naturally, with all the speed and acid that was already in my system from the few days past. It turned out to be a decent night all around, sitting back, bullshitting, and combing the beach area. Salisbury Beach was pretty well mobbed on a hot summer evening. Coming from one party in Lawrence to another in Salisbury, I was pretty well lit for the evening indeed!

I decided to head back to the clubhouse a little earlier then the other brothers wanted too. I took the old river road back; it was always a nice winding road to ride on. While I was riding through downtown Haverhill, I got the bike winding at 60 miles per hour, passing a rice grinder—a Japanese bike—running into a pot hole the size of a sewer cover. It must have been about a foot deep, and at the speed I was traveling, my top triple tree cracked right off the spindle and lowered the bike a few inches. I pulled over to the side of the road to check out the damage. I was lucky I didn't lose my front end completely. I would have done a somersault through the air, probably would have broken my back. I said to myself, just take it nice and slow, keep an eye on the front-end, and hopefully make it back to the house. As I rolled in, my prospect Dennis was sitting out front with a few babes. The music was blasting. He laughed with a smile, as I was maneuvering the bike nice and slow, heading to put the bike into the garage. "Parco, this is the straightest I ever seen you!" he said, as he kept on laughing. I guess I was, since I was hanging on to dear life. I was pretty well lit for the night. I got off the bike and headed to the refrigerator for a cold brew to mellow out and get ready to go upstairs to crash. I realized later—that was a sign post that I ignored, to slow down all around the board—not just riding, but life in general. But I guess I was too preoccupied with the "Live Fast—Die Hard" routine in which I was eventually on to, then again, already hit head on, but didn't notice it.

Quick Nick came onto Snake and myself about distributing some felonious twenty dollar bills. The three of us got together to go down to his business outfit. We made our choice on which bills we wanted to attempt to cash. They were all printed slightly different. We sorted through them and took the ones we thought were easier to cash. Nick didn't give the offer to anyone else in the club, since we were the ones who operated it. I'd have my prospect Dennis attempt to cash some for me. One afternoon, Dennis, his ol'lady and I were taking a ride around the city. As we were going through an intersection, a cop was directing traffic. Dennis yelled out the car window "officer, can you change a twenty?" He was laughing at the same time. I came down on him since I was a little paranoid. It went in the cop's ear and out the other. He just kept on directing traffic. Dennis was always joking around. He laughed at the whole matter.

During that time, I was constantly going into altered states. Too much speed on top of the hallucinatory drugs I was inducing was doing it. Alcohol and narcotics also footed the bill. I'd her voices one day, the next I'd be back down to surface level. When I would be hearing voices, they would be so vivid and real. It was like having a conversation inside my head with who ever I was hearing. I was working at a machine shop out of Lowell. I'd go to work on speed, riding my Harley. One morning, I lost my license plate and the cops pulled me over and wrote me up for anything they could dig up. They stated that I better head back home or else they were going to radio in to the next city ahead. I took their advice and headed back to the clubhouse. I made a plate and headed to work the next day. A couple of other workers had some Jap bikes. At lunch, we would get together to go for a quick cruise along the Merrimac river. One of them worked adjacent to me. After a while, the noises from the machines started to get me. My head started hearing voices, the voice of the one who worked next to me. It was like an argument of some sort. I was almost ready to hop over the machine to beat his head in. Instead, I got up, punched my card and walked out. That was the end of that job. I went back to the clubhouse for the weekly meeting. The brothers noticed that I was starting to lose it. Flipper, a new prospect, told me "Parco, think of the lord, think of the spirits." It was all getting so bizarre, indeed. We had our club meeting. After that, Nick, Zap, and I started doing some weight lifting. We were discussing getting into a regular regime to get into better shape. We were all shooting the breeze.

As Nick and Zap decided to leave, I decided to have Nick drop me off at my father's house to get some good shut-eye. My head felt finally clear. Just as Nick was dropping me off, the voices started creeping up on me. I got into the house and upstairs to my bedroom to crash. All of a sudden I started hearing sirens and cops inside my head. I thought that they were coming in the house to bust me for the funny money.

I was hearing, "All right, were coming in to bust you for those fake twenties!" Then I'd hear my father's voice saying "Get rid of that money, now!" This went on repeatedly for about an hour. Talk about paranoia, the next thing I was doing was lighting up the funny money to ashes. I let them burn on my bedroom floor. They went up in a flash. Once they were disintegrated, so were the voices. I could roll over in bed and finally crash. That was some experience of insanity to reality.

Nick along with some native Indian he met went up to the horse racetrack to get rid of his funny money. I believe it was definitely the wrong place to try to do so. They have the feel of money constantly since that is their primary part of the job. They wound up getting busted on the ordeal. I don't recall what the outcome was, since he didn't go for the hearing till we were both out of the club. I passed him in the court house as I was handling one of my own ordeals.

I'll never forget about one of my lady friends that were a fantastic artist. She did a beautiful hand painted piece of nostalgia on top of my gas tank which was glossy black, along with the rest of the machine. It turned out to be a scaled serpent with wings, the details and colors individually placed in their proper position. The scales of the serpent were green, black, and gold, while the wings were white, outlined in red, with some gold tracing the red. Beside it was "Evil Spirits M.C." in a stylish, yellow painting. It was just what the doctor ordered. She was married. But her husband worked the night shift, so we didn't have much of a problem connecting with each other. We had some good times together in bed. I would always be high on some felonious substance. She was just naturally high from her art work. She would always be smiling, with large pupils of her eyes, staring directly into my eyes, like trying to follow me.

11

West Street Story

The last time I scored with my artist female was one hell of day I'll never forget. We were in the sack all afternoon. Just finishing scoring, we headed downstairs to grab a beer from the refrigerator. As we were walking out of the house to the front yard, a bunch of the brothers were planning on some sort of joint venture. They were surrounding Nick's step van. Zap yelled to me to come along. They had some furniture to pick up for the clubhouse. I gave my girlfriend a kiss goodbye, telling her that I would see her later. I hopped into the van and while we were riding, I got the lowdown on what was happening. Some dude that Zap knew was in hot water due to some dealing with some Puerto Rican junkies. He sold them a bag cut with baking soda—a large bag at that. And these spics were going to do a number on him big time. So he was moving out of the area completely, giving us some of furniture in exchange for helping him leaving the premises. When we arrived at his apartment, I could see a group of Puerto Ricans gathering, pointing towards us. I gave them the finger, and went with the brothers to start clearing out the apartment. Coming out of building, two car loads of spics pulled up. They got out of the vehicles, opened their trunks, and pulled out tire irons, car jacks, and two-by-fours. I stood out in front of the brothers, wanting to drop kick one of the mutha-fuckers, but there was another right aside of him. Just with that notice, I got struck in the head with a two-by-four. I headed in back of the step van, to get the cobwebs out of my head. The dude that we were doing the moving for was hightailing out of sight. I decided that I'd get back into the rumble. All hell broke loose. Zap was out there, swinging a machete around. Nicky was swinging his cane. That was the last sight that I could recollect. I got hit in the head again, this time, a car jack. It struck me so hard that I went into shock. All I could remember next was that I was standing in the Lawrence Police Station with Preacher. The cops were the ones that came down to break up the riot and arrest a couple of the junkies. This all came about on

West Street in Lawrence. Whenever I hear about the movie West Side Story, it all seems to blend in. Gang fighting, Puerto Ricans, and so on.

After signing the police forms, we headed out of the station. Nicky was out front, sitting in a borrowed vehicle from one of the hang-arounds from the clubhouse. We got in the car. Nick went to start the car but the battery went dead. Some Spanish women were walking from the station. It was their husbands that got arrested. We asked them if they had any jumper cables. They stated that they were returning to the station and that they would have some. We waited about 10 minutes, and they returned in another vehicle and the men they were with, gave us the jump we needed.

We drove out of the parking lot and headed towards North Andover where I had a date waiting for me. When we got to an intersection, the light was red. A Hispanic pulled up aside of our vehicle, and his passenger threw a bottle through the window at Nicky, hitting him in the head. They took a left hand turn, we took a right. Nicky told us to hold on, making a 180 degree turn, stepping on the gas pedal to the boards, heading towards the rear-end of the Puerto Rican vehicle. BANG! We hit them so hard we sent them onto the lawn of Honeywell Corporation. Our front-end was totaled, but still running. Another car full of spics started chasing us. Nicky had his head out the window, since the hood of car was folded up to our windshield. Preacher and I were helping Nick, doing the navigating to lose the other vehicle that was following us. When we were able to come to a complete halt, we got out of the car to get the hood back down from the windshield. Somehow, we made it back to clubhouse in one piece.

Snake was on the roof on the porch with a loaded shotgun. I was determined to go pick up my date for that evening. Even though I was running too late, I was hoping that she would still be waiting for me. Nick gave me a ride in another vehicle, but it was too late. She already split. When we got back to our house, all the lights were out. Zap was walking in front of the building with the shotgun in his hands. I started feeling a lump on my head, along with some chronic pain. I went into some altered states, going to the other brothers to have them feel the lump on my head. I decided to head upstairs to my bedroom and decided to crash after dropping a couple of downs to curb the pain. I remember getting undressed and hitting the mattress, waking up the next day to head downstairs for more painkillers. Some of the brothers from the Canadian chapter were down visiting, along with some members from the Charter Oak M.C. from Connecticut. I was just hanging out the window, since everyone was out front, partying, and reached my hand out to receive a few downs. Off I went, back upstairs to my bedroom to crash back out on the mattress. I found out much later that by the third day after the brawl, my sister came down to the clubhouse to see what was happening with me, since she hadn't seen me all week. When the brothers told her the lowdown, she immediately had the brothers get me dressed, and had them bring me to her place so she could get me to the hospital.

12

Life After Death

No one knows the blues like I do. Either that or they're dead. I woke up in the intensive care unit. My head was draped completely with a gauze bandage, not a hair left standing on my head. My brother-in-law was standing beside my bed. I had to take such a wicked piss, but I couldn't do it laid down. My brother-in-law told the nurses that he would walk me to the bathroom. They agreed and up on two feet I was, ready to piss in the normal fashion. Shit, there were times that I would be speeding my ever loving mutha-fuckin' brains out and unable to piss, more or less needing a righteous piece of ass to clean my tubes.

When I returned to my bed, I was told the complete history of my operation. The doctors thought I was goner. I had a massive blood clot in the temporal lobe of the brain, along with a massive fracture to the skull. The clot was so large, they didn't know at first if they had to operate on the other side of the brain. I was able to comprehend what was happening, but was unable to express myself completely, verbally. The words just wouldn't come out. The doctors didn't know if I was going to get over that obstacle. They were more concerned with the fact that I was still alive after such an ordeal. After the neurosurgeon came out of the O.R., the doctor told my family that everything turned out successful. Jokingly, he said that he removed all the "evil spirits" from my head.

The club had some party over that weekend. There were complaints to the police by the neighbors next door. It was one of the most rowdy weekends the club ever had. The brothers let me know that a window was shot out of the neighbors' house after the police answered their complaint. By the beginning of the week, the Town of Methuen sent a building inspector that decided to close the premises, due to faulty wiring.

When I got out of the hospital, I went to the clubhouse. It looked like a cyclone went through it. I could feel the emptied feeling inside of me and the living room where I sat. Not a soul in sight. I went up to Salisbury Beach. Walking through the center, I ran into some biker friends I knew. They were amazed in seeing me bald they were use to seeing me with my hair past my shoulders. I explained what happened. They were kind of dismayed over the whole ordeal.

Was this the end of the club, or were we at a standstill? It was all too vague to understand. The next thing I knew, the clubhouse burned down to the ground. Was it from the faulty wiring, or did the Hispanics wing a Molotov cocktail through one of the windows? Did the president have a contract to have it torched? I'll leave it to the reader's discretion. What does it matter anyway? It was finished. Snake and Geronimo turned in their colors. When the going gets rough, the tough gets going. Going out of the club was their motto. What got me was especially Snake, who started the club with me in the first place. He should have stuck it out through thick and thin. We didn't think too much of the situation, since we were still doing fairly well after all of the bullshit we went through.

I sold my bike to Dude, since I needed to get it out of my father's cellar. My father was completely bullshit over my brain operation. He wanted me out of the outlaw biker scene and he figured it was going to turn out to be getting worse then better. Once I had a new apartment, I grabbed another scoot to build into a chopper.

We started having our weekly meetings up in Haverhill at Preacher's apartment. I decided to go up to Lowell to talk with Hook and a couple of other Angels. As I was walking up to them, they looked at me in surprise! They were wondering what the fuck happened to my head—my hair used to reach past my shoulders. Now I was bald with a horseshoe shape incision on the right side of my temple. It stuck out like a sore thumb. Hook seemed to be staring right at the injury, like "what the fuck?" I explained what happened. Hook was still dismayed. I told him that we wanted to have a club get together at Koza's Café in Methuen. He said that they would be game. We made it for the following Saturday night.

Everything seemed to be going about cool. The brothers were active and ready to party. Hook, Hawkeye, and Fuck-Up, along with about a dozen members, some from out of state, made it to the Saturday night get together. There was a live band on one side of the bar, so a lot of brothers rotated from one side to the other, or just out front of the club to get some breathing air. A couple of Methuen detectives pulled up out front, called me over, asked if there were any problems. I told them we were all set and off they went. Nicky sat down with Hook and Hawkeye. Hawkeye was downed out. He was starting to nod, while Hook and Nick were having a serious conversation. I'd go outside with Fuck-Up and a few other members to smoke a joint and talk about the injuries we've been through. Fuck-Up was in a full body cast. He broke his back from sliding underneath a tractor trailer truck while riding his Harley, the one he bought from Zap. I told him about the riot I was in and how I got my head smashed. All in all, it turned out to be a fairly decent evening. When the Angels were getting ready to split, Hook gave me that same dismayed look he gave me a week ago, when he first noticed my head injury. He was a very suspicious outlaw himself. That's how he was, probably from all the injuries he sustained in the past. They all left with positive vibes, quick and abrupt, like military style.

Since our weekly meetings were up in Haverhill, we started bar hopping downtown at the Lido Café, and the Chit Chat Lounge. As a few months went by, I noticed a change in my attitude due to my head trauma. I thought about it for a few weeks, and finally I came to a decision. Still as vice president, I decided to pack it in and resign. At the next meeting, Nicky, as president, decided to hang it up too. The club kept on rolling with new authority to operate from. I started hanging with a speed freak that lived down the street from me, getting stoned and boozed up. It all got too boring after awhile. I contacted the brothers, telling them that I wanted back into the club. I attended the next meeting which they were going to make a decision on the outcome of the status quo. I sat in the kitchen until they called me back into the meeting for their view on this issue. After one of the longest meetings the club ever had, they called me into the living room with a "welcome back" attitude. I was a member again, but with less seniority than before.

13

Your Ol'Lady, My Ol'Lady

A lot of crazy shit was going down, especially on the relationship with women. As I'm going back to the start of the club, one of my first, fairly steady encounters was Susan. I mean, there were broads left and right of me, a quick piece, and off they went. She was a sort of country girl, living out in the wooded area of Andover. She was Black Foot Indian and French, with blond hair, blue eyes, petite, with Indian cheek bones. She loved riding on the back of my chopper. We would do some LSD together and would go on a nice long cruise on my bike. One night, I decided to stop at my sister's apartment to use one of her bedrooms, so we could score for the evening. My sister and her husband were always cool people. I'll never forget that evening. The LSD was called windowpane acid, it took you to a nice peak, then slowly it would taper off, you would be able to still feel some effects of it the next day. The sound of her having an orgasm that night is still embedded in my head. I believe they call them pussy farts. Well, her pussy farted all right as I fucked her. I almost fell in love with her. I'd pick her up and we would be riding with Snake and one of his little babes. She was ready to come live with me, and I was game, so we rode up to her place to pack a suitcase. Snake was aside of me on his scoot with his ol'lady. While we were waiting for her to come out of the house, Snake kept on hounding to me, "Come on Parco, we should split." He finally talked me into it, so we scooted off, leaving her behind.

Another problem came up about a year and a half later. Snake ran into her again, and she claimed she had my daughter. He laid the word to me, had her address where she was living on her own, and said she wanted me to stop by. One night, when I was good and stoned, I had Snake drive me to her apartment, to see what was really happening. It was a wrong move. As I walked into her place, two dudes were sitting on her couch, while she was in bed with some other character. When I walked into the bedroom, the dude jumped out of the bed, and headed for the door. There was no child. The crib was empty. I told her "Get dressed, you're coming with me." I was tripping on acid. We got into Snake's car and had him drop us off over at my place so everything would be cool and we'd be able to be alone with each other. I walked her to the bedroom, I wanted to lay down, get comfortable, and take it from there. "All you want is a piece of ass" she stated, and got up out of the bed, then split. I followed her out the door, but I couldn't keep up with her. I guess it wasn't meant to be.

I was spending some time in the Boston-Cambridge area, due to the fact that I had my trial pending in the Cambridge Superior Court on that Assault & Battery with a Dangerous Weapon charge I had from that 74 North Reading party bit I was involved in. I'd meet my brother Dude for lunch in downtown Boston, since he was working in that area. He had a beautiful Japanese woman named J.J. that was living in Boston which I met in the past while he was scoring with her. I told Dude to put in a good word for me, that I was attracted to her, and was looking to spend some time with her if she was willing to comply with me. She said that she did like me, so Dude would bring her back from Boston, and we would hit it off from the first date. After that, it was up to me to drive into Boston to pick her up for the night. We would usually get high together on some speed, and screw our brains out for the evening. She was the first piece of ass I had that introduced me to sodomy, and man did she love it. I'd be ready to start screwing her doggy style. She would grab my dick and say to me "Up the ass, Parco, up the ass!" By morning, I'd be all set to give her a ride back to the city. I'd give her a couple of grams of speed to get rid of for me.

Everything seemed to be going cool with her for a while, 'til other females would start turning my head. I would start scoring with another babe named Chickie. She was as tall as I was, and as slim as a rail. She was a really cute gal, but for some reason or another, I'd just use her for a past time. It seemed impossible to find true love in those days, only a few babes I would go crazy over. I took her to the 76 New Years' Eve party at the Lido Cafe in downtown Haverhill. She was an easy-going gal to get along with. We would get up to boogie together on the dance floor, right through the evening.

The music group was getting ready to bring in the New Years' cheer. As the drummer started walking up in front of the bandstand, I wound up snapping from all the agitation I'd been holding in from my brain surgery. I blew a short circuit, so they would say. I started to go after the drummer. Dude grabbed me and sat me back down into my seat 'til I came back to my senses. Chickie looked at me in shock, wondering what the fuck was wrong with me. The guys in the band didn't know what to make of it. Then, everything went back to normal. We partied 'til the end of the night.

There were so many different babes I was going with, I kind of lost track of what I was doing with half of them. If I wasn't seeing Susan, I'd be seeing Nancy. If I wasn't seeing Nancy, I'd be seeing a different Sue. If I wasn't seeing Sue, I'd be seeing J.J., and so on and on. It was the Sue that split town with the other gals that really drove me crazy, not the one that had my daughter. I was really interested in marrying her. It seemed close, but no cigar, so they would say. Before her it was Linda, a California gal. She loved to get high. When we split up I went totally insane over her. There were a lot of other women that I scored with, but they were Bam-Slam-Thank you-Mama situations. Most of the women I went with were on and off relationships. We'd separate for months, reconnect somehow and before you'd know it, we were lovers again.

During the year 1976, I started scoring with a gal named Emmy. She was American Indian and Italian, with two children. She was about ten years older than me, but really hip. I met her years back, when she was living with an Indian fellow, named Pinto, from the Pleasant Point Reservation in northern Maine. They were next door neighbors from my brother Butchie's apartment. We'd all get together and party at one apartment or the other. Pinto eventually had some warrants in Lawrence. He decided to head back to live on the reservation. So when we started seeing each other, it seemed like we were hitting it off together—pretty good after a while.

When I first tried to pick her up, noticing her walking down the street, she would get scared and run up the street to her apartment. After a few tries, I got her into my car, and from then on, we would hit it off. I wound up getting an apartment right down the street from her. She would come down and party, and end up in the sack with me for quite some time.

14

Mandatory Gun Law

I was working on the other bike that I decided to chop. Everything seemed to be working out fairly decent after awhile. I had a neighbor in my building that set me up with some dude that had access to some large quantities of Valium—by the thousands. Life seemed like it was turning around for the better once again. I spent more time in bed with Emmy than most of the other chicks I went with, probably due to how many Valiums I was swallowing. Sex in bed was like brushing your teeth. It turned into a daily ritual. My neighbor, Gary, was another crazy fucker. I'd be wheeling and dealing with him. I went up to the Lynn chapter of the Angels to see if they would be possibly interested in any Valium. They were all set in the narcotics field, but were interested in some uppers at the time.

One evening, I decided to throw a party with the brothers and a few friends that hung with us. Emmy wore a mini-skirt that evening. My friend Chucko brought a stranger with him that night who was three sheets to the wind. As he would be walking by my ol'lady, he'd lift up her skirt. She would come over to me and tell me the situation. I kind of let it slide and told the dude "Hands Off." He didn't listen, and attempted to do the same thing again. Only this time, I was seeing him in action. I grabbed him by the neck, and threw him out bodily. Preacher booted him in the ass, while I gave him a knuckle sandwich. That took care of his perversion pretty quickly.

By the end of the night, I decided to earn my Red Wings. My ol'lady was on the rag, so I went down on her to eat her out in front of the bros. Dude thought we were bullshitting, so Emmy flashed her rag right in front of his face. "What do you call that, huh?" she flashed. Zaps ol'lady was also on the rag that weekend, so they competed with us, so he could earn his Red Wings. They proved their point. Everything seemed to be going cool, indeed. That was some wild night, but most of our partying nights were always wild, whether orgies, gang bangs, burning out, fighting, or just going for a crispy bike run.

On a cool autumn night, Zap and I would decide to take a ride down to Hartford, Connecticut to party with the Charter Oak M.C. We first met them when they were making their annual run up at Salisbury Beach one summer. We became good friends. They previously came up to our clubhouse, so it was vice versa, out of state for an over-night good party. As soon as we arrived, I got a nice line of crank. Then one of the members took me out to a nightclub. I was pretty well lit. The speed was pretty potent and the club was packed. We'd listen to the band while having a few drinks, head back to the clubhouse. A couple of lines were waiting for us, just enough to straighten out my act. Speed was funny. Sometimes I would feel like I was over amplifying, and then, another line would just straighten me out. We would be talking about whatever came to mind. The next thing you'd know, the sun would be starting to rise. We got a good share of speed to bring back for the other brothers to get a buzz on. We made sure our colors were off our back, since otherwise driving down the highway at six in the morning, we'd stick out like a sore thumb. In a few hours we would be back in Massachusetts. No problem.

Since we were making Haverhill our new stomping grounds, usually after bar hopping for the night, we would head over to Preacher's apartment to start a card game with a time limit for 6 am. Since we were all up on speed anyway, it would be a good past time. I'd be on a winning streak, up to about the last half hour. Zap would be starting to pull the winnings in. We already set the time limit, but since he was starting to bring in the bread, he would want another half hour, then another half hour, to make up for his loss. That was Zap, he always had to win. We would finally call it quits, so we could lay back, relax and mellow out for the new day to come.

We were considering finding a new place to rent for a clubhouse. We were having pretty good vibes on keeping the club in operation even though we lost quite a few members since the Spanish riot. While I was still seeing Emmy, and getting all the Valium I wanted, my neighbor Gary got me out of bed around two in the morning to give him a ride to his local supplier. I was half awake and half a sleep, I must have had a 100 milligrams of Valium in me. I was eating them like candy. I finally came to my full senses while I was sitting in my car, waiting for him to return from what ever he was up to doing.

All I wanted to do was head back to bed and crash. He came out of the building and back into the car. Off we went. I went through a blinking red light without stopping. Who was on the road in the middle of the week after 2:30 in the morning anyway? You guessed it! *John Law!* Pull over, you're busted. I was just in the process of transferring my registration, since it was a new car, but it came out of the computer as an unregistered, uninsured vehicle. The next thing I know, a single barrel shot gun comes out of the back seat of my car. Gary had thrown it in there, without me even knowing it! This was the first year of the mandatory gun law of one year in jail, if convicted. We were both charged with possession of a firearm. When we went to the police station, sitting at the table, answering questions and emptying our pockets, Valiums started rolling down the table, while the detective was filling out the arrest forms. Lucky enough, I caught them with my fingers and popped them into my mouth before he lifted up his head. Other than that, I thought that he didn't want to see them anyway—he was content with this gun charge. The rest I kept stuffed in the bottom of my pocket.

While we were waiting for arraignment, I passed out a handful of Valiums to the fellow comrades who were waiting court procedures. I wanted my pockets clean just in case another search was to take place. When they transferred us over to the Lawrence House of Correction after bail was set, I contacted Emmy, so she could get in touch with Preacher to give him the lowdown to come bail me out. I ran into my good friend Papa Gino. He was awaiting a drug trial. After a few hours, I was out of there. So was my neighbor Gary.

I didn't see the shadow of defeat heading my way. I was just too fucked up to give a shit. When we got back to our apartment building, Gary and I started getting fucked up, big time. We were killing a quart of vodka, screwdriver style, on top of the Valiums we had already eaten. His girlfriend Moe was friends with the Susan I was madly in love with, and had her over that day at her apartment. We all went out in the backyard. Gary and I started a game by tossing an egg back and forth. With each catch, you take a step backwards to get further apart from each other. Who misses the egg, loses. I was on top of Susan, pleading to her to marry me. Emmy was back at her apartment, but she would be down later in the afternoon. But I didn't give a rat's ass, I wanted Susan. She finally gave in, and agreed to marry me, but by the end of the day, she changed her mind. See what women will do to you?

After my name made the newspaper, my landlord came into my apartment while I was in bed with Emmy. One of the brothers let him in the door. I just stayed in bed and listened through the keyhole for what he had to say. He noticed the Harley that I was building in the living room. I heard him complaining that the bike shouldn't be inside the apartment. I just stayed in bed until he left. We were planning on getting an apartment together with her two children anyway, since it was getting to be a hassle for her to be running back and forth to her place.

We finally got a new apartment up on Tower Hill. A fellow biker that I knew was my next door neighbor across the street from me. As we were doing the moving, Gary told me that another guy named Pinto was looking for Emmy, and that he was carrying a knife, so watch it. He was Emmy's former old man. Sure enough, he made it over to our new apartment. I took him across the street to talk about the situation, man to man. I also had a knife on me. I told him he was welcome to party with us. I grabbed the knife I had and threw it into the ground. He followed and did the same with his blade. Then we went arm and arm, back inside to party for the night.

Tonto was over with his ol'lady to help us move in. We were having a good time. 11:00 was starting to creep in, and I mentioned last call to the package store. Pinto decided to take a ride with me. I was pretty well lit already. On our way back, I noticed a nice Sportster sitting out in front of a bar. I told Pinto to hop out of the car to grab the machine. He said "Not me brother!" So I told him to take the wheel of car and meet me around the corner. I hopped out of the car, and headed for the bike. It was facing a downhill position, so once I got it rolling, I was able to get on the seat and roll down the pavement. Pinto was sitting behind the wheel, right where I told him to be. I had a blanket in the car. We used it to wrap around my arm and the steering wheel of the car while I sat on the bike to pull me up the hill. It was like being glued to the driver's side off the vehicle. My new apartment was on Tower Hill, so it was an all uphill battle. We wound up driving a couple of streets passed the one I was living at. It was my first night there, plus, I was pretty well lit to begin with. I let go of the blanket, and rolled down the hill, going pass the street I lived on. I got off the bike and started pushing the machine back up to the street I was living on. By the time I made it to the front of my apartment, I was out of breath and sweating my balls off. Tonto helped me get the bike into the apartment. I headed to the bathroom, took of my T-shirt, and stuck my head under the faucet of the bathtub, drenching my head with cold water. What a fuckin' crazy night it turned out to be.

15

The Back Stabbing Begins

The next day, I went completely insane. For no specific reason, I turned Pinto on to his ex-ol'lady, mainly to the fact that I was preoccupied with my own ego, my machine. We became blood brothers by cutting each other's wrist and wielding them together so the blood would interchange between us. Since I was going to make a good size fast dollar on the bike I ripped off, I'd have enough bread to finish building the machine I was working on. I went down the cellar to see if I could hot wire my telephone in my apartment, but, no go. Paranoia seemed to start creeping inside me. I started hearing voices all over again. Dude comes in riding on the machine that I sold him with one of the French sweat hogs the brothers already screwed. He wanted to use one of the bedrooms to get his piece of ass from her. I told him not today, we were just getting situated. I didn't want anybody outside of the club seeing the bike I ripped off. The owner of the bike was French Canadian himself. Loose lips, sink ships, and I didn't want to go down. I felt that I was going to make it back up to where I was before I had my brain surgery. That night, I had a buyer, but the fuckin' bike wouldn't fire up, it wasn't getting any spark, even though I hot-wired the ignition. What a fuckin' bitch. I told the buyer to give me another day. He agreed, but he never made it back the next night. If I had it running the first night he was over, he would have been riding off with his ol'lady on the back of the machine. What a bummer. I started sleeping over Tonto's apartment so I could have some space to feel more at ease with myself. I called up Zap, but he wasn't in. His ol'lady's cousin answered the phone. He told me that the owner of the machine that I ripped off was offering a $200 reward for the whereabouts of his bike. I didn't think too much about it, how he got the information and all, 'til later on the next day when I went back to the apartment and found out both bikes missing and Pinto was gone too. Emmy gave me the low down, that the cops were over the night before and confiscated the bikes. Pinto had a warrant on him, and so on, and so on. I headed to the police station to at least get my machine back, but they just ignored

61

me, like I wasn't there. I thought Pinto was the culprit that set me up. When I got back to the apartment, Emmy explained to me in details that it wasn't Pinto to blame, but my own brother Zap. From the word I got about the reward, everything seemed to fall into place. It had to come out of one specific horse's mouth. The cousin wouldn't have known anything other than overhearing Zap talking to his ol'lady about the ordeal.

Luckily, I contacted a captain on the police force who knew me personally through my family. He was aware of all the shit I've been going down under, the riot and all, and had my charge reduced to receiving stolen property instead of grand theft, which would have been a felony. I got my own bike back from the basement of the station except for the sissy bar. When they picked it up, it was already apart—engine out of frame, front end and real wheel off and so on. I couldn't complain about a "dime-a-dozen" part that I could replace easily.

Pinto showed up after hiding for a few days. From becoming blood brothers, before all this turned into a hassle, his arm started to infect, he used salt pork on the area to heel it. I felt sorry. It was like cause and effect, since I thought he turned on me, my blood went sour on him. Since the case was clear, we started partying together for a few days. I had a boa constrictor, from my former neighbor, Gary. He gave it to me during our drug transactions. I named the snake Meth. Pinto and I attempted to drink at a bar and I had the snake around my neck and over my shoulders. The owner of the bar told me to leave the premises. He didn't like the idea of the snake being in his bar. I ignored him and refused to leave the bar. He called the police and they came down and pulled me in for protective custody. Just as they were walking me out of the bar, Pinto grabbed the snake on my shoulders and went back to the bar to drink. The owner just didn't like idea of an outlaw biker feeling at home in his domain. I had to do four hours in a cell cause of that, but that was just the start of more bad karma I was about to face.

Pinto started hinting to me to come up to live on the Pleasant Point Indian Reservation, north of Maine. I thought of it, but I was willing to stick around for the consequences I had facing me. He asked me if he could borrow my car to go see Emmy, and he would be back within and hour or so. At that time, I was crashing here and there. I was staying over at Heavy's apartment. As the night went on, I was wondering what was taking Pinto so long to return. I got a ride over to Emmy's apartment from Heavy to see what the hell was going on. She told me that he took the dog, Maggie, and said that we were both heading up to the reservation. He took off up to Maine with my car, the bastard. I was fucking bullshit.

The next day I had to go for a preliminary hearing on the motorcycle caper. I pleaded guilty to receiving stolen property. I was completely bullshit over the whole situation. Getting set up and ripped off by a brother I prospected into the club, and a close friend. Don't get me wrong, I was into a lot of dirty business of my own, but I never did it to betray a brother or a close friend.

That evening, we had our scheduled church meeting up at Preacher's apartment. Dude picked me up, Zap was with him. I was still in my dress clothes, taking care of business all day long, going to court and seeing my shrink. While we were riding up to Haverhill, I started rambling on to Zap. It was about how I heard that he ratted on me, and I was going to bring it up at the meeting. He got pissed off, and told Dude to pull over. He wanted to start a rumble with me, since he didn't want to hear the truth at church. As we both got out of the car, pissed off, I was in no mood to jam. I just turned around and started walking the other way. Dude was no help. He was too fuckin' crispy anyway. Imagine, both brothers that I prospected in, didn't respect me like they did from the start of their membership. If I was in Dude's shoes, I would have got into the middle of the situation and have it settled at the meeting. I was bullshit, as I walked across the street I gave the traffic stop sign a front snap kick. At the same time, I was thinking psychologically of stabbing Zap in the back, he was a two-faced-mother-fucker when I finally got to really know him, the other brothers didn't hang with him as much as I did. I just left the club, not one of brothers tried to contact me to know what actually did happen. I guess it was a blessing in disguise, the club was eventually going to hit rock bottom. They say the Lord works in mysterious ways. Well, I guess that's true.

'Invictus' by William Ernest Henley, 1875

Out of the night that covers me,
Black as the Pit from pole to pole,
I thank whatever gods may be
For my unconquerable soul.

In the fell clutch of circumstance
I have not winced nor cried aloud.
Under the bludgeonings of chance
My head is bloody, but unbowed.

Beyond this place of wrath and tears
Looms but the Horror of the shade,
And yet the menace of the years
Finds, and shall find, me unafraid.

It matters not how straight the gate,
How charged with punishments the scroll,
I am the master of my fate:
I am the captain of my soul.

16

It All Goes Down

What I heard was that the club members were eventually going down like the domino effect. Lenny got killed in a motorcycle accident. He was one of the easiest going brothers in the club. There was a big write-up in the paper about the incident. Zap started throwing stretchers along the hospital floors when he heard that Lenny didn't make it through the ICU. They put together a righteous, biker funeral for him, with a couple of other clubs attending. After that, most of the other brothers decided to pack it in. Zap decided to go all the way into the Hell's Angels. Dennis was also another member that decided to go H.A. Preacher had a new prospect, Barney, but from what I heard, they were the only two left flying the Evil Spirits insignia. Zap had the Angels close the Spirits completely by rounding up all the colors from Preacher. It was probably the right thing to do. The club really was finished after the Hispanic riot, but our self-centered ego still pressed on to keep it operating.

My former neighbor Gary and I had our possession of a firearm dismissed, since it was registered under his ol'lady's name. He used the excuse that we were out earlier target practicing and when we got back to our apartment building, he thought that she took the firearm up stairs, vice-versa. I just got convicted of an uninsured vehicle out of the whole ordeal.

I pleaded guilty to receiving stolen property for the motorcycle caper. The judge gave me one year probation.

I was found guilty of assault and battery with a dangerous weapon in 1977 from the 1974 stabbing at that post Halloween party down in Reading, Mass. I didn't have any witnesses due to the fact that my trial was delayed from the brain surgery I underwent. The brothers that were going to witness for me either skipped town running from the law, or had their own charges waiting to be heard. Zap used the excuse that it wouldn't look good on his behalf since he was flying H.A. colors. I was sentenced to two-and-half years in the house of correction, suspended to four years probation, with the stipulation of three months in the Billerica House of Correction to be served. It was a crazy three months to handle. I was still recovering from my brain surgery. The judge that sentenced me was Dude's father. What a small world it is. Before sentencing, he let me walk for a couple of weeks, I was on personal recognizance. Another biker might have split, but I figured this was the last of the bullshit I had facing me. I just partied before going in to do the time. I felt like I was floating on cloud nine. As Jumpin Jack's favorite saying was "In The Ozone—In The Ice Land—On A Cold And Windy Day—Like Yesterday—Watch Out For The Ice!!!" In another sense, I can think of all the positive aspects I achieved. I've sowed most of my oats, not all, but quite a few.

The fascist regime is rising. Pull over. They want to see where you're at, what you're doing, more or less, the ol'lady expected you home an hour ago. Better off staying in and getting a good buzz on. Well let's not get into this—too heavy. Because a shot of—or a puff of—would do you fine right now.

I ran into Preacher and his wife shortly after I got out of jail. They were in a van in a shopping mall parking lot, so I hopped into the van and started to talk about what's been happening. They lit up a joint and laid some bad news to me. Their son, Shawn, got hit and killed while riding his bicycle out on the street. He was like family to me. Before club meetings would go into motion, I'd be playing around the house with his son. I can still visualize those days when there was nothing but fun. "Hey Batman, hey Batman," he would say, and I would answer, "Yes Robin," and we'd be chasing the imaginary villain across the floor. Well, I take it that he's in heaven now. He didn't have to suffer the grudge of the day at a time living. He was blessed, that's the way I see it.

Zap decided to give Preacher an unexpected visit—a crack on the head and the rip-off of his Harley shovelhead, along with a little help from his friends. When I heard the lowdown, I didn't consider that to be too fuckin' cool. I was told that Preacher was treated for a fractured skull. I guess Zap figured if he could do one brother in, since no more status quo, he would do another in. Preacher went bullshit and decided to retaliate. He went looking for Zap at one of the biker bars in Lawrence with a loaded handgun without a license to carry. When he entered the bar, and what actually went about inside the joint was beyond me, but he did get busted and convicted on the one year mandatory gun possession law. Luckily, he got sentenced to do weekends, since he was working and he had a family to support.

Butch was found guilty of possession with intent to distribute methamphetamine. He was busted by selling a couple of ounces to an undercover narcotics agent. I believe he got sentenced to four to six years in Walpole State Penitentiary. He would have burnt out sooner or later if the law didn't straighten his ass out.

Snake got set up with possession with intent to distribute THC. Jumpin Jack sold him the stuff, then plea bargained with the State Narcotic's Bureau to beat some rap he had hanging over his head by letting them know of Snake's drug dealing. Zap convinced Snake that he could set him up with a lawyer that would keep him from doing a day in the jailhouse. Zap must have got his share of the sum that Snake had to pay for that defense. He was convicted and sentenced to one year in the Lawrence House of Correction.

While Snake was awaiting trial, I decided one night to go party at the King of Clubs dance club. I noticed Zap on the other side of the bar with another former Evil Spirit, Wilkie. I walked over to see what was happening. The next thing I knew, Zap sucker punched me in the face. Without any thought, I came back on him three-fold and knocked him on his ass. Wilkie got in the middle of the fight to save his own ass, or Zap might have come down on him after the fight. The next thing I knew, the detailed police officer grabbed me by behind, and walked me out of the club to my vehicle. Zap was following right behind us with about a dozen busybodies expecting an outcome of the situation. The cop got me into my car and off I went. I decided to stop at Snake's house to tell him what had just happened. My knuckle was bleeding, so I must have got a good punch in on the sucker. Snake was happy that I got the best of him, since Zap was fuckin' with him in other ways, before Snake's drug bust.

Here is the low-down on Lenny's fatal accident.

CYCLE CRASH KILLS 2 July 19, 1976

Amesbury-A weekend party for motorcyclists ended in a crash, death and a near-riot early Sunday night.

Police Chief Edmund J. McLaughlin linked the party at the home of Albert R. Reed, Jr., 2 Whitehall Road, with the death of two party-goers, an assault in a Friend St. establishment, two arrests and an unsettling scene in Amesbury Hospital.

Twenty-one members of Amesbury, Salisbury and state police organizations were called to quell the outbreak of disturbances and keep the motorcyclists in check.

Leonard Michel Goudreault 22, of 561 Amesbury Road, Haverhill, and Mrs. Brenda E. Wilson, 19, Carriage Hill, Amesbury were killed.

Dr. James F. Whitten, medical examiner, said Goudreault died from multiple fractures of the skull, chest and legs.

Mrs. Wilson was in critical condition in the intensive care unit in Amesbury Hospital until about 12:30 this morning, when she died. She suffered fractures of the skull, neck and chest.

Police said Goudreault was driving a motorcycle at high speed on Whitehall Road, between a quarter and half mile from Reed's house, when he hit the rear bumper of a car driven by Miss Linda M. Dylingowski, 28, of Boston. The accident in front of 90 Whitehall Road, happened at 6:33 p.m.

Miss Dylingowski had just backed out of a driveway after visiting relatives and was heading toward Friend St. at slow speed when the accident happened.

Police said Goudreault and his passenger, Mrs. Wilson, were thrown a distance as a result of the impact.

Police could find no evidence either motorcyclist was wearing a helmet.

Nearly 60 motorcyclists were guests at Reed's party that started Saturday night, McLaughlin said.

Became Beligerent

He said approximately 30 motorcyclists gathered at the scene of the accident and became belligerent.

Another group of motorcyclists, numbering about 25, went to Amesbury Hospital.

McLaughlin said the group at the hospital became "unruly and belligerent" when they learned about the death of their companion, Goudreault.

There were reports a table in the hospital was overturned.

Several police officers were dispatched to the hospital to restore order.

McLaughlin said some of the motorcyclists were "under the influence" from the weekend party.

He said they returned to Reed's house and then went downtown. A disturbance followed, resulting in the early closing of Friend St. taverns.

McLaughlin said a patron of Albert's Pub, Friend St., John Blodgett, Hilliard Road, Kensington, N.H., was cut above the left eye with a broken beer bottle. He reportedly was slashed because he was not mourning the death of Goudreault.

Blodgett ran, bleeding to the police station and was taken to Amesbury Hospital in the fire department ambulance. Six stitches were taken to close the wound.

While in the hospital, Blodgett told authorities his car tires were slashed. The car was parked in front of Albert's.

McLaughlin then ordered the Friend St. bars to close. Salisbury and state police were sent to order all patrons to leave the establishments.

Police are seeking a motorcyclist nicknamed "Dude" in connection with the assault on Blodgett.

Ending the Party

Amesbury police went to Reed's house, told him to take his family inside, and ordered others to leave the premises, ending the party.

While at Reed's, police arrested Raymond Bowman, 39 of 11 1/2 Mill St. and Richard Goudreault (no relation to the man killed in the accident), 31 of 106 Friend St., both of Amesbury. They faced disorderly conduct charges today.

Salisbury police sent six officers with the paddy wagon. They were Officers Gary Lattime, Gary Ingraham, Forrest Hunt, Dennis Champagne, Charles Merrill and Edward Foote.

State police responding to the call for manpower were Troopers Ted Harvey, David Peterson and Stephen Gravelle.

Officer Richard L. Peeke and Registry Inspectors James Rau and David Pierce of the Fatal Accident Unit are investigating the accident.

Goudreault was born in Haverhill, June 3, 1954, son of Leonard A. and former City Councilor Marjorie E. (Ryan) Goudreault. He worked for the Haverhill Department of Public Works and was a member of St. John the Baptist Parish, Haverhill. He was graduated from St. James Grammar School and from Haverhill High School in 1972.

Besides his parents, he leaves four brothers, Steven, Patrick, Christopher and Matthew Goudreault, and four sisters, Barbara, Ann and Mary Goudreault and Mrs. Julie Parker, his maternal grandparents, Herbert L. and Mary A. (O'Sullivan) Ryan, his paternal grandparents, Ernest J. and Leona (Poirier) Goudreault, all of Haverhill, and several aunts, uncles and cousins.

The funeral will be Wednesday morning at 9 from C. Frank Linnehan and Son Funeral Home, 129 Kenoza Ave., with a Mass at 10 in St. John the Baptist Church. Burial will be in St. James Cemetery.

Calling hours at the funeral home will be Tuesday from 2 to 4 and 7 to 9 p.m.

"Reprinted with permission of The Haverhill Gazette"

Lenny was one hell of a good brother. He was the type of guy that went with the flow, party and ride, and he never looked for trouble. He was always a close member with the club. He was the first of the brothers that wound up in what they would call "Harley Heaven."

Dennis was one of the brothers that prospected for me. He was already connected with some Lowell Hell's Angels so he fit the position as another tight member. When the going would get rough, he would be right there with no questions to ask. We had more fun partying together, especially when we were doing speed. One evening a former member of our club, Ronnie, was holding a party and invited us over. Well, during the party, another so-called friend of the club started wise-cracking about the club. It seemed all in fun, but Dennis took it seriously. We were the only members at that party. Dennis asked Mark if he wanted to "go at it" out on the street. Mark was always looking for a fight. He was the brother of another former member, Wilkie. Ronnie told me "Don't interfere. It's one on one." I had to agree, we were out numbered anyway. Dennis was game. Mark came out with a few of his karate kicks, then down on the pavement they rumbled. Mark got the best of him. The fighting stopped. Staring back at each other Dennis said "I'll go at it one more time with you!" They went at it head to toe. Even though Dennis lost the second round, he proved his point.

He eventually went Hell's Angels. Before that in his last days with the Spirits, he had a hassle with some off duty police officers. Here are the newspaper articles about it.

THREE OFFICERS FACE FIVE DAY SUSPENSIONS Sept.25, 1976

Five-day suspensions for three Haverhill police officers were recommended yesterday after testimony they broke down a door and dragged a man into the street and made him take down his pants while they were off-duty.

At a public hearing in City Hall, Mayor Lewis C. Burton took the case under advisement. He has 48 hours from the time the hearing ended to make his decision.

The police officers were not in the city council chamber to hear the stories told about them. With their lawyer, they left at the start of the hearing, the lawyer saying there had been reports the mayor had "pre-judged" the case.

Charged were officers Peter J. Ryan, James E. Smith and Donald C. Apitz. They were charged with offenses against Dennis J. Ring, 123 Cedar St., at 1:30 a.m. Sept. 24.

The recommendations for the five-day suspension were made by Det. Capt. Daniel M. Fasulo, who investigated the complaints. He said Deputy Chief Richard J. Sheehan concurred in the recommendations.

Ring said a man he later identified as Officer Smith awakened him that night, banging on the door of his apartment and asking about "pot" for sale. When he disclaimed any knowledge of marijuana and asked who was there, Ring testified, he was told a "girl named Pat" sent the man.

When he told the man to go away, Ring said, his door was kicked in, a man entered the apartment, twisted his right arm behind his back, forced him to the street, pushed him against a Volkswagen and removed the denim shorts he was wearing.

Ring said his assailant claimed to be from the FBI and that if he resisted he would be charged with assault.

When he reached the automobile, Ring said, he recognized Officer Apitz, with whom he had gone to school. Apitz and the other two men were in civilian clothes, he said.

Ring said his girl, Donna Bodwell, called the police station and a cruiser arrived a few minutes later. He was released, he said, and was asking the three officers for their badge numbers when two uniformed officers got out of the cruiser. He asked if he was under arrest, and when he got no answer, he walked away.

Ring said he made no complaint to the cruiser officers, but later went to the police station and talked to Capt. William C. Poock. He was advised he could go to court to make a formal complaint, but said he wanted to make a complaint within the police department, which he was allowed to do.

Officers Americo Colletto and Richard Noury, who responded to Cedar St. in the cruiser, were called into the station and Ring said they were not the ones who were involved with him.

"Reprinted with permission of The Haverhill Gazette"

3 OFFICERS SUSPENDED Oct. 15, 1976

Suspensions of one year, six months and three months have been imposed on three police officers for involvement in an assault and disrobing incident on Cedar St., last month. Appeals are expected.

Officer James A. Smith, 30 Woodland Way, Merrimac, was suspended for one year by Mayor Lewis C. Burton.

Officer Peter J. Ryan, 111 King St., Grovesland, was suspended for six months and Officer Donald C. Apitz was suspended for three months.

Each was found in violation on the following charges. Conduct unbecoming an officer, conduct injurious to the peace and welfare of the public, violation of certain laws of the state, and violation of a citizen's civil rights and the Constitution of the United States.

Burton found there was insufficient evidence to find any of the three guilty of intoxication.

According to testimony at the hearing Tuesday, Smith was identified as the person who kicked in the door of the apartment of Dennis J. Ring, 123 Cedar St. at 1:30 a.m. Sept. 24, twisted Ring's arm, forcing him outdoors to Cedar St. in his shorts and socks.

Ryan was identified as being in the corridor of the house when Smith kicked in the door.

Apitz was identified as being outdoors, on Cedar St., when Smith and Ryan emerged with Ring.

All three, according to the findings, were involved in making Ring place his hands on an automobile while they removed his cut-off dungaree shorts.

The mayor said he would have no further comment on the case.

It is expected the officers will appeal the suspension to the Civil Service Commission. They have five days in which to do so. Then the commission has 10 days in which to set up a hearing, and there must be a report on the hearing, to the commission, within 30 more days.

"Reprinted with permission of The Haverhill Gazette"

17

Lockup Sucks!!!

Three months in the Billerica House of Correction for something that I didn't do was more than just a joke. But an additional two and a half years suspended to four years probation was like putting the icing on the cake. The first couple of weeks were in the maximum security. You had your own cell to relax in, a gym to work out in, a library and the yard. It didn't seem that bad 'til I got transferred to the minimum security, which was called the dormitory. I thought it was going to be okay there too, since half of the inmates that were on weekend furloughs came back on time half blitzed. They were able to make it back in without even being searched!

Some big dude came back from maximum security. He was well known. He supposedly screwed up before and was sent back to the Max to make up for it.

Well this so-called big dude was nothing more than a fudge packer. The side he was on was where they were into fucking each other. I ended up getting transferred to the side he was on. And it wasn't like the double bunk side. Instead, it was a "three to a bedroom" side.

How I found all this out was because he wanted me to join the fudge packing team. I told him I didn't think so! But he kept on insisting. I told him I couldn't even get a hard on! But he advised that I'd go into my room and try to get it up with a sock over it. Well luckily one of the screws came by just as I was going to attempt to get a hard on. If you can't make it, it was a fake it ordeal. He had me sent to the maximum security where they put me in the infirmary overnight—at least to relax. I stayed in the maximum security for a few weeks. I was bullshit about the whole scene that went on at the dorm and I told them my share. Sure enough they ended up searching all of the maximum security. I don't think they did a damn thing over at the dormitory. The guards were calling me chief as if I was helping them out. All I wanted was peace of mind. My lawyer got the parole board to okay an early parole for me due to the fact that I recently had brain surgery and I would be prone to sustain another serious injury in that area until the doctors put a plate inside the skull. The board agreed on the early parole.

In between time, I got sent back to the dormitory to do my time. The guys there got on my case that I'd have to give in to the fudge packing group. After a while I got fed up with the bullshit. One night during supper one of them edged me on into a fight and all hell broke lose. The guards broke up the fight and sent both of us back to maximum security with charges. Number one, fighting; number two, creating a disturbance; and number three, refusing to listen to an officer. When I went for my hearing all I told them was "You wouldn't want someone fucking you up your ass would you?" I got locked up for fifteen days.

Word floats around the House very quickly. Nothing is hidden while you're in jail. The majority of the inmates were in my favor. They gave me the nickname "Sock man." It was what started the whole incident.

While I was doing the 15 days I got my early parole paperwork to sign and mail out to my mother. I gave it to a guard to mail for me. It may have ended up in a barrel. When my lock-up days were finished, I called my mother and she said she never received the paperwork. I was pissed. She had to contact a friend on the police force to go through the process all over again.

The inmates were bullshit over having their cells searched. They ended up starting a ruckus by setting the mattress shop on fire. This is where inmates worked during the day for mere cents. A bomb was made and thrown into the yard at a prison guard. It caught him by a hair and he made off without a serious injury. As days went on, the inmates trashed the library, flipping anything they could get their hands on. The warden thought the House was getting out of hand and called an entire lockup before supper in the maximum security. The inmates were bullshit. They threw whatever they had to burn into the halls of the tier and yelled, "Light 'em up," and the whole jail house was on fire. That went on for ten days including some tiers smashing their sinks and toilets. The last 5 days of the15 day "lockup" were getting better than worse. The inmates had most of their aggression released and simmered down quite a bit.

That two week ordeal was one hell of a time. I had the inmates next door to me call the guards saying that I had a fit and I'd lay there with the shakes and they rolled me into the infirmary so I could relax and cool off for a few hours. It was one hell of a riot the inmates stirred up while I was there.

I started reading a book on Chinese Philosophy that an inmate lent to me. I almost got through the entire book by the time I was able to walk out of the damn place. It was just another time filled with obstacles to contend with.

18

You Talk the Talk, You Walk the Walk

After that time in jail, I was hanging with a good friend, Rick Mall. Rick was a party animal. We would get together and party day after day. He lived right around the corner from me. We were walking from Broadway Liquors one night and we ran into Zap helping his stepbrother settle some dispute. Jimbo was a cool dude. He wasn't into fighting, just partying. But someone was giving him a hassle, and Zap coached him into fighting his way out of problems. Well it looked like he got his ass whipped but stood up for himself with his fist instead of mouth. There was blood left all over some black man's van. Jimbo went up to his apartment and started smashing the windows in his apartment. I ran up to kind of calm him down and get him out of the apartment and back on the street. When I got him to cool down and out of the apartment, the black guy was standing next to his van. He acted as a wise ass and told Jimbo to clean the blood off his van. Zap didn't like that and I didn't think it was the right time for Jimbo to do anything except to chill out. It turned out that Zap got into a scuffle with the black guy and Zap got the best of him. We headed to his ol'ladies car just as the police were arriving. She threw it in reverse and she was able to out beat having to explain to the cops. We took a ride up to Haverhill to visit Barney, a former Evil Spirit prospect. I broke open the six-pack and we talked a bit about old times.

It turned out that an arrest warrant was put out for Zap for Assault and Battery. Zap contacted me over the whole ordeal and asked me to witness for him. I went to court with him to testify but it didn't help. The cops were after his ass. He got sentenced to the Lawrence House of Correction.

To make matters worse, I had just got my license back and was having a good time once and for all. The cops who put Zap in jail were out to hang me for whatever they could get on me. I was drinking at a bar in South Lawrence early in the evening and they were driving by the club while I was standing out front to

74

get some fresh air. When I decided to leave the club and get in my car the cruiser was right on my ass. They pulled me over and busted me for driving under the influence. I wasn't even drunk! And they knew that. They just wanted to bust my balls. I asked not to have my car towed, and they agreed. I went to the police station and took a breath test, which I should not have. Usually the cop's word sticks before yours anyway. The bail bondsman was there within a half hour. I was able to walk to South Lawrence Bridge to pick up my car. Luckily it was still there. I hopped in and drove it to my apartment. Talk about busting balls! A friend I had that worked at City Hall knew the cop. He and I together met the cop while my friend asked him to lay low on me as a favor to him. But when court came he didn't change his way. The Judge gave me ten days in the Lawrence House of Correction. The cop was pleased with the result.

The ten days in the Lawrence House of Correction was a joke. I knew a few of the guards from past experience with the Y.M.C.A. and Junior High. One would talk to me on the graveyard shift. The place really sucked. There were two or three in each cell with a fuckin' bucket to shit in.

I had the mayor send a letter in to put me on the county farm. The days were like months in there. There was a class action suit filed during the ten days, for which I was the plaintiff. Judge Garrity claimed it unconstitutional such as cruel and unusual punishment. I was able to do time with little problem. There was a gym upstairs that didn't even have a roof on it. At least we were able to do an hour workout after supper.

After a few years went by, our lawsuit got settled. We ended up with $20 for each day we were in. Two hundred dollars from jail is like hitting *Ed McMahon'*
Sweeptakes.

After the Spirits were no longer in action, one of the former members decided to start a new club. Geronomo was the type of member that when the going got rough he would turn his colors in. He was a member for a couple of years before he decided to give it up as a member. I don't know whether his ol'lady drove him to do it, but he did it anyway. The club was really rockin' at that time.

Geronomo started his own club and he named it "The Gravediggers." I would talk to him at the Horseshoe Lounge and felt impressed seeing the new colors in the city. I was tempted to join the club, but I would flash back on my past with the Evil Spirits and the reason why the club eventually dismantled.

Well it goes like this. It's usually all the way or nothing at all. After Zap made it into the Hell's Angels, I had problems with other bikers that I didn't even know. But they knew of me.

I started working at City Hall, custodian, second shift. I had a hard ass boss that would get on my nerves. By the end of the night I'd head to "Dirty Eddies" to mellow out with a few drinks to cool my jets.

I heard that The Gravediggers opened up an after-hours bar. After "Eddies" called last round I decided to check out the new club. Heavy was there, along with a former member from the Pallbearers M.C., Bobby G. Bobby G. was always a good shit to rap with. He could talk as fast as a natural speed freak. Heavy was an old friend from before the Spirits even began. I knew him during the sixties. He was drafted into the Vietnam War. After his first leave after basic training, he went *A.W.O.L.* He ended up doing 90 days in the brig and came out with a Dishonorable Discharge.

The night went on and I had a few drinks talking to the bar maid and another old friend I got into partying with. All of a sudden Geronomo made a 180 degree turn on me and accused me of trying to put the make on his ol'lady, the bar maid. He was no longer with his former woman from the Spirit years.

"Fuckin' with my ol'lady, huh?" He and another member of his club started throwing me around. The door opened and they threw me down a flight of stairs. That wasn't good enough since I was able to land on my feet on the bottom of the stairway. They rushed down the stairs, and we started pushing and shoving and then they turned around and walked back into their club. I got into my car and noticed that they had John, the hippie that I was talking with at the bar, out on the street. It looked like they wanted to start a fight with him from hanging with me. I decided to drive around the block and back in front of the club to see if I had to help the dude if they started swinging. It seemed that they let him walk, but at the same time another biker that was hanging with them, threw a beer bottle that ended up landing on my windshield and cracked the damn thing completely. I was fuckin' pissed.

I stopped at the Lawrence Police Station and wanted his ass grassed. I got into the cruiser and we headed down to the club site. The cops wrote up some complaint that would have to end up going to the court's magistrate. At the same time the cops said that I'd have to leave my car in the station's parking lot because I had too much to drink. I only lived a mile up the street and it was about 4 in the morning. That didn't interest them. They wanted me to come back after shift change to pick up my car.

I walked around my apartment obsessed over the whole matter. I've been crossed by the system a few times before. I thought they were going to have my car towed to a garage and I'd have to pay the storage fee. I decided as the sun rose, to walk down to the station and pick up my car. As I was driving out of the parking lot, sure enough the same cops that drove me home were pulling in the lot, flashing their lights on for me to pull over. That was it. I ended up with a driving under the influence charge.

I lost my license for a year. I talked to the Alderman of Public Safety who I knew very well. He used to be a sergeant for the police force that arrested the Puerto Ricans that almost killed me with a car jack. He wrote a letter to the registry to help me get my license back after I explained to him what happened.

I ended up attending the magistrate office hearing. He agreed with the complaints and filed them for a court hearing. After Geronomo and his buddies left the court, I talked to the magistrate personally and after all that time waiting for the hearing, I cooled down enough to let them get away with what they had done. He agreed with me since it was my decision and dropped the charges.

It was close to being a year without a license to drive. I usually would hit the bars on Broadway or clubs around the city to drink and pass time. The Gravediggers knew that I dropped the charges on them, but I was told that one member was still after me over the whole ordeal. I didn't think much of it, I had threats before this.

One of the members that I knew told me that "Bones" was pissed off at me and that I should watch out for him.

Well, I would party from club to club on Broadway, The Wonder Bar, Middleton's, The Theater Club and the French Social. There were a few more too. There was nothing better to do in the City of Lawrence but hit the bars.

I decided one evening to hit a dance club out of downtown. I ended up partying and ran into a chick that was hot to trot. It seemed like a pick-up and sure enough we ended up leaving together to go over my place for the night. I got into her car. We were already half buzzed and she asked me if I had anything to drink at my place. I told her no. So she came up with the idea of stopping at The Gravediggers after hours club to pick up a bottle. She parked her car and left me sitting in the vehicle. After ten minutes I figured I should pop in to see what was keeping her. Naturally she was floating around the club. Bones spotted me and asked me what I was doing there. My former bro, Preacher, was there and yelled out to Bones, "Leave Parco alone, he's not doing anything." Next thing I know it was a Déjà vu. The door opened and I got pushed down a flight of stairs. I decided not to land on my feet that time, but fell on my back. That didn't please the dude. He came down with two other friends of his and they started chasing me down the street. When I stopped running, Bones started fighting me. I decided to throw the fight since there was three against one so I let him get the best of me. I was knocked unconscious. When I came to, the cops were all around their clubhouse. The chief that I knew was standing in front of his car. I told him I wanted him to shut the place down or I'll have the State shut them down. They rushed me to the hospital for treatment. I had some broken ribs and a few other abrasions. The next night the Lawrence police raided the place and had them closed down permanently. Eventually, the club dismantled and no longer flew colors. See what women will do to you!

19

Unexpected Surprise!!!

Well, time went on. Not knowing what to do with myself, I decided to go back to school for some type of degree, or just pure knowledge. That's when it all happened. I ended up running into my daughter with her mother in some business office building. It couldn't have been anything more than a shock to me. But again, nothing is an accident except the possibility of another obstacle hovering in front of you. I'm an optimist. I see things as the here and now. Not yesterday. Not today. I have to attack this typewriter head on. It's not easy, but once I get going, fuck it all. Just start. Hitting the buttons work as a relaxing response therapy.

Well, my daughter and her mother stood out like a sore thumb!!! These buttons are getting pushy. I'm starting to get a little punchy, but what the fuck? That's life. Come out with the punch if you still got it. Where was I, oh yea, we ended up meeting with each other without her knowing who I was. Imagine that? She was the same person, same attitude, just a little bit wiser.

I'm coming back to the conclusion that nothing is sacred. Only the dead are living, a rebirth that some go through on this plane in life.

When we got to introduce ourselves, I asked her if her name was Sue. I told her that my name was Frank. She acted like she didn't recognize me because she knew me by my nickname, Parco. I realize now that she was only playing me. I told her that I remembered her from the old motorcycle days, at the Calumet Club where all the bikers used to hang around. She was formally dressed, and so was I. I didn't have the long hair and beard I carried when I went with her in the early seventies. Looking at my daughter was like looking into a mirror. She had the dark hair and eyes I have. Her mother seemed free-spirited, with her mind already preoccupied since she'd recently got married. She asked me if I would like to follow her over to her place so we could talk about old times. I agreed, and met her down in the parking lot. As we were driving, my daughter was waving back to me out of the hatch-back window, like she already knew me from the past.

Talking about the past, I ended up breaking up with her when she decided that she wanted to come live with me. She didn't know she was pregnant at the time. And my brother Snake talked me out of the idea at the last minute, just as she was packing her suitcase. She lived in the sticks in the rural part of Andover. Snake was seeing Linda at the time, who eventually became my girlfriend. I fell in love with her as soon as we started going together. She was the girl with faraway eyes, originally from Stockton, California. It was life in the fast lane during that time.

We finally arrived at her apartment, beautiful area, nice and peaceful. When we got inside, she told me that her husband was sleeping, he had to work third shift. No problems.

"How long have you been married?" I figured I'd asked her while she was lighting up a joint.

"A couple of months now, we were living together for about a year before we decided to get married. He treats me great."

"How old is your daughter?" I figured I'd ask her just so there would be no question that I was the real father.

"Five. Her name is Elenora May, Ellie May for short from the T.V. show, *The Beverly Hillbillies*."

I was thinking what to ask her next, wondering whether her husband was going to wake up or not.

"Have you seen any of the bikers lately, Snake or anyone?"

"Yes, off and on. How about you—have you seen anyone from the past?"

"No, I've been dancing at different clubs all through the country as a stripper. I came back to Massachusetts and met Danny. I decided to be a housewife instead of working. I get everything I need. I haven't seen any of the old friends from the past.'

I couldn't believe my eyes, sitting down watching my daughter while her husband was in the bedroom sleeping, knowing me as a total stranger. I figured it was time to cut the mustard so to speak.

"Susan, I'm sorry to tell you this, I'm Parco!"

She looked at me with total illusion, wondering what was going to come out of her mouth next.

"That's right I didn't want to shock you all at once." It was Ellie that made me go this far as to even follow this conversation from the start. It was exactly the higher powers of the Cosmos that made this happen the way it intended to be.

"Oh, Frankie, please don't ruin my marriage. My husband wouldn't have married me until I convinced him that you were doing a life sentence in jail for murder. He has a daughter of his own from his previous marriage and he figured you would eventually come looking to see Ellie."

She was more serious than I thought, especially with her husband home sleeping through all this without waking up.

"What about Ellie? I'm willing to pay child support. She's my daughter. I want to start seeing her regularly."

"You can see her anytime you want. All you have to do is say that you're my cousin," she persisted.

I didn't know what to think, how her husband wouldn't be able to recognize that she was my child, not her mother's cousin, and how my intellectual gut level was going to handle it all.

I decided to let her have it the way she wanted it to be, the fact being that that my daughter was doing so well. I figured that it would be better on her behalf, but my nervous system took a heavy toll.

I'd usually wait for her husband to leave the apartment to head for work. I'd go up to see Ellie. Her mother didn't mind at all, even though it would be 10:30 P.M. She would wake her up for me, just so I could feel like my real self once again. It caused a lot of heavy drinking in the process.

I finally met her husband in the oddest predicament. While I was working at City Hall in Lawrence, Sue, Danny, and Ellie came walking through the hall to have Ellie's last name changed to Bergeron on the birth certificate instead of her mother's maiden name. This way they would be one whole family. I was standing in front of the office I was working out of, and Ellie comes running up to me to tell me the good news. Danny and Sue were right behind her. Sue introduced me to Dan as her cousin. He believed it and I went along with it. How it went about was beyond me, but he shook my hand and then they went into the records department to make it all legal.

As time went on, I'd end up running into Sue working back at the dancing profession she supposedly gave up. She would be on a night off, hanging with another dancing partner. We'd talk, shoot the breeze, and would call it a night. Another time I'd run into her walking downtown with some other sugar daddy, not even saying hello to me, just giving me a quick eye contact flinch.

We finally lost contact with each other completely. Her phone was disconnected. I decided to stop trying to get in touch with them. As I rode by their apartment, I could see that it was vacant.

Finally one Saturday morning, I got a phone call from her. I was really shocked, surprised, and dismayed after she gave me the low down on what was happening and how come she hadn't been contacting me. She told me that she went on a fling with some other dude, left Danny over it, and ended up living in the projects in Lowell. She told me she made a big mistake with this other guy, since he was abusive and she broke up seeing him. She was back talking with Danny and she explained the whole situation to him that I was not in jail and she was in contact with me. But everything was all right. He had nothing to worry about. She gave me her new address and invited me to come over anytime. I went over and met Danny for the first time with nothing to hide behind. We ended up being good friends. We started going out together, Sue, Danny, and my girl-friend. It turned out to be too nerve wracking for me. I'd dance with Sue, and she would tell me how much she loved me, while Dan would be dancing with my girlfriend. By the end of the night, I'd be half in the bag, we would go party in Lowell, and crash over her apartment.

When I would go over her place alone, she would tell me that she was unde-cided whether she was going to go back with me or Danny. She finally decided to go back with Danny, figuring I'd be too possessive. They got a new place and got all the furniture they had out of storage. And then she decided to dump Danny for all he had. She was still dancing at different nightclubs, and found another relationship. Danny was bullshit!!! I was still able to pick up Ellie on weekends, but she wouldn't let me through the front door.

She ended up making another move with her new encounter. I wound up catching her dancing in the combat zone of Boston when I just made a move into the city. She didn't want me picking up Ellie, since I was living in Boston. I think she was on her own guilt trip.

One night I went down to the Zone to look her up since my family was going to have a surprise birthday party for my mother turning 60 years old. She gave me the okay to pick up Ellie in front of a drugstore in Lowell.

The party went well. On the way back to Lowell, Ellie wouldn't say a word and looked very depressed. I had to drop her off where I picked her up. I didn't think anything of it 'til later. Her mother didn't want me to know where they were living.

That was the last I saw of both of them. I went to the post office to try to find her new address, but no luck. She must have had a P.O. Box all along. I'd see Danny, and he was in the same boat that I was in, only worse. She got possession of all the furniture he owned.

That was the last time I spoke with Danny. We lost contact with each other over the years. I started working at the Attorney General's office and stayed on for four years. When I started there, an attorney I worked with said he'd help me find my daughter's whereabouts. It turned out that he just took advantage of the situation since I was getting more wired than normal over this situation. He seemed to enjoy it, since I was getting everybody else on their toes. I finally told him to drop the investigation after two months not doing a damn thing. I felt more relieved that way.

After the four years working with that department, one of the criminal investigators I became very friendly with listened to my problem. Within fifteen minutes he called me over to give me Ellie's stepfather's address. After I left the administration, (another story to itself), I was able to find her stepfather. He told me that they were living in North Carolina. Sue gave up dancing and worked in a business position, and Ellie was doing fine. That was 1991. I haven't had any contact with any of them since.

It seems that life takes its toll on many folk. Sometimes you just have to keep it in the middle, erase the I. Come out with "We or Us or Them."

20

Starting a New Life

While still living in Lawrence, the Hispanics were kept on their side of the turf and the white population kept their control of the city. It was the damage of my brain injury that sent the vibrations across the wave length of the astral plane that kept fear in the atmosphere. When I'd be walking down Broadway, the Hispanics would look the other way, catching the vibes I had about what had happened to me. I was trying for a permanent city job, but was told to sit tight and something would come about. My patience has had it, and when I got accepted as a tenant in a subsidized building in the heart of Boston, I didn't give it a second thought but to make the move.

When I left the City of Lawrence in 84, I left it powerless over the paranormal connection with the Divine. I headed to live in Kenmore Square, Boston, the heart of the city. There was more non-stop partying then you could imagine. The building I lived in was six stories high, close to a hundred apartments. Once I got to know over a handful of tenants, I didn't even have to leave the building to party. I met a former stripper that had a stroke, but she was a pretty babe even though she was semi-paralyzed. I'd go over her apartment to smoke a joint, and for a $20 spot, she would put out for me. I had friends to drink with, coke with, or smoke with. It was some way of living. By the time I'd make out to the clubs, I'd be half-lit already. One of the security guards that worked the grave yard shift, Andrea became my steady girlfriend. I'd talk with her for hours after making it home from partying all night. It was life in the fast lane all over again.

While watching the news at the beginning of August, a riot evolved in the City of Lawrence. I felt like I was right back at the scene. It all started with my former next door neighbor Gary Gill, who got me busted for possession of a firearm. Here is the write-up from the Boston local newspaper headlines.

NEW RIOT HITS LAWRENCE Aug.10, 1984

Dozens of people were injured and at least 11 arrested last night as rioting broke out again in Lawrence between hundreds of Hispanics and whites.

Shots were fired and Molotov cocktails, rocks and bricks were hurled from rooftops at police.

By early this morning about 200 state police, a SWAT team and officers from surrounding communities, carrying rifles and shotguns and using dogs, drove the Hispanic group from the riot scene.

The officers then swarmed into the grounds of the rundown Essex housing project and chased the rioters into the buildings. Their presence forced an uneasy truce.

Hundreds of whites who had challenged the Hispanics on Oxford Street had drifted away or were forced by police from the scene.

Earlier in the evening on Oxford Street, about 40 Lawrence police and the SWAT team, outnumbered by the jeering crowds, drove back rioters by firing tear gas.

Other officers charged forward, clubbed the rioters and dragged them into awaiting cruisers.

The injured, holding towels to their faces to stop the bleeding, were hurried away to waiting ambulances at the scene.

A state of emergency was declared by Lawrence officials. Police cars cordoned off the Tower Hill area where trouble had broken out for a second night in a row.

At least 11 people aged 18 to 25, were arrested last night in charges of inciting a riot and disturbing the peace.

"The main problem now is a lot of curiosity seekers who are trying to incite," said Lawrence Ptl. Ray Smith. "This will be going on all weekend."

"This isn't over by a long shot."

Last night's trouble began following an outdoor religious service held on Oxford Street, near a liquor store that was fire-bombed during the previous night's violence.

The service was held to calm racial tensions. But when it ended, hundreds of Hispanic men formed in one section of Oxford Street and hundreds of whites banded together at the other.

The Hispanics began beating on garbage cans and they and the whites shouted racial slurs at one another.

A line of Lawrence policemen moved in across Oxford Street between the two groups and minutes later, Molotov cocktails were hurled through the air at both the police and the white group.

Sgt. Leo Ouellette, commander of the Lawrence police tactical unit, ordered his officers to fire teargas at both groups to break up the explosive situation.

Police Lt. Norman Duggan and his partner were on Oxford Street when two Molotov cocktails were thrown and narrowly missed them.

"Then a guy came out of nowhere throwing sticks," said Duggan. My partner got hurt. It just missed me."

His partner, whose name wasn't available, was later treated at the hospital.

Patrolman Walter Soriano, a Hispanic officer, said, "In the 14 years I've been a cop, I've never seen anything this bad."

After midnight, the army of police had been assembled on Oxford Street ready to drive the Hispanics back to the Essex project.

But suddenly four Hispanic men came forward to bargain with police.

"We've got everything settled down and then one guy started up again," one of the men told three police officers. "They don't like this crowd of police. They're scared."

One of the officers told him, "You have 10 more minutes. We're not stopping once we start. We're tired of playing games."

At 12:20 a.m., the police drove the Hispanics into the project and inside the dilapidated buildings.

The Essex Housing Project is considered the toughest in the city and has been the scene of much violence over the years.

After police had cleared Oxford Street, the scene looked like something out of Beirut.

Bottles and rocks littered the pavement and the windows and fenders of a car parked there were battered and smashed.

One onlooker, Jose Santiago, 35, said, "This is just craziness for no reason."

One teenager, asked why he was there, said he just wanted to be part of the excitement.

Joe Levesque, 18, said, "We came out to protect our grounds, to protect what is ours. They're the ones throwing firebombs, they're the ones with the guns."

Howard Johnson, 27, said, "This is what you call an all-out war. It's bad, very bad for the City of Lawrence."

Police and residents said the first wave of rioting Wednesday night that raged for five hours to the early hours of yesterday was caused by a smashed windshield that unleashed tension between whites and Hispanics.

Residents charged Wednesday night's incident escalated out of control because police retreated when two cruisers were stoned after initially responding to the street fighting.

"The hoodlums own the street," said Jim John, a retired mechanic who lives next to Pettoruto's Package Store, which was looted after it was firebombed.

"The cruisers backed out and let them fight it out among themselves."

John was among dozens of area residents who complained that their repeated calls for police protection went unanswered for about two hours.

But police officials yesterday defended their decision to lay back while assembling reinforcements, including stage police and members of a regional SWAT team.

Lawrence Police Sgt. Bert Baker said if the 10 Lawrence police officers on duty at the time were sent to the scene, "they would've been killed."

And Sgt. Leo Ouellette said that a "strong show of force" was needed to quell the riot, so that sending in officers piecemeal would have been useless.

By the time the SWAT team marched into the riot area around 1 a.m. yesterday, the violence had just about ended, witnesses said.

Police said the violence began as a feud between two sets of families and friends, divided almost evenly into whites on one side and Hispanics on the other.

Bad feelings between the groups had simmered for weeks, and police said they erupted Wednesday evening after a car windshield was smashed.

Of the 14 people hurt in the violence, five sustained wounds from random shotgun blasts fired into crowded street corners.

Two people remained in the hospital last night.

A liquor store and an attached two-story home were burned out by some of the dozens of Molotov cocktails, which were hurled during the height of the five-hour riot.

Hundred of people from the tough Essex projects located a few hundred yards down Oxford Street then got into the fray, police said.

Seven people were arrested, including a man who allegedly stoned two State Troopers and a police dog that were among an 80-member SWAT team called in.

Dozens of witnesses told The Herald the windshield smashing stemmed from an even earlier incident when a young Hispanic boy kicked at a dog belonging to Gary Gill, 31, whose house was later firebombed by marauding rioters.

Gill was taken into protective custody by police.

Witnesses said after the little boy kicked at a fence where the dog was barking and snapping at him, the boy was "slapped around" by a man as dozens of bystanders watched about 5:30 p.m. Wednesday.

"Reprinted with permission of the Boston Herald"

After that riot, a majority of the small businesses and apartment buildings went up in flames as the years went by. It was said that the city of Lawrence was one of the most fiery infernos in the United States. Diane came along one winter day and I thought I might have had a decent relation going. The ethnic population is mainly Hispanic now, and it is one of the largest heroin distributors in the Commonwealth of Massachusetts.

21

Just Screwed

It was like trying to find a needle in a haystack, just another day out of life routine. My so called relations with the female gender seemed progressing. Andrea and I were living in separate worlds. After her abortion of my child, we were seeing less of each other as time went on. It was going from once a week to once a month. I figured Elissa was a fairly out going woman, so we kept a good strong relation with each other. It seemed that it wasn't the answer to all my mishap illusions. Diane came along one winter day and I thought I might have had a decent relationship going. She had more than one hang-up though. That was her problem. They say the number three is completion. And sure enough completion came to a standstill.

I'd consider getting involved in one strong drunk or another. As Hunter Thompson stated, "I wouldn't recommend sex, drugs or insanity for everyone, but they always work for me" and that is what seemed to be to be the final conquest. Without it, I felt empty inside. No bitch could actually satisfy my sexual desire, not the ones that I was seeing. I've been thinking of a lot of serious bullshit because that's where it all comes down too. Life sucks, fuck the world, live for today, that type of routine. The karmic state was still running on the negative side. I've been through enough sorrow and hardships. As long as I had some wine and some women that was the ultimate. Ultimate was the final conquest of the grim reaper, and certainly, I was a grim reaper, an Evil Spirit. Yea!

It all came about one evening on a date with Diane. I was trying to manipulate with the flow, but the flow was going so strong, I just decided to let it go and see where it would come out to be. Before picking her up, I digested a couple of valiums along with a quarter of a pint of 100 proof peppermint shnapps just to get my adrenalin stimulated. We went to one social party, to start I had a few drinks and decided to split. We headed to my stomping grounds, Kenmore Square, The Rathskeller. The bartender poured me a couple of double shots on the house, with a couple of beer chasers to cool my jets. We stayed to last call, headed down the square to hit the Pizza Pad. With one slice of pizza, you could buy two pitchers of beer, such a deal. By the time we were headed back to my apartment, I was in a black out-oblivion, not knowing what the fuck I was saying or doing. This is what I was told what happened that evening; Diane had her hand on my thigh while we were sitting in my living room. I replied to her, "What the fuck do you think you're doing, jerking me off?" You see, we never fucked before, but she gave awesome wicked head. She would end up swallowing the orgasm, keep on sucking on the mother fucker till it was hard again. It was great, but I was an intercourse man. Well she got up and split. Without thinking I called Elissa, and off I went, three in the morning. The next thing I know I was sitting in the State Police Headquarters, not knowing how I got there or why. The arresting officer told me that he stop me at Interstate 93. He told me to get out of the car, which I did, and attempted to arrest me for driving under the influence of alcohol. I stated to him that I wasn't drunk, and headed back to get into my car. He called for back-up from two other officers. They got me into the cruiser and off to the station. I was at the headquarters where I became fully conscious. I was bullshit wondering how I was going to get out of this mess. They wanted a breath test from me. I told them to bring me to the hospital, since I was headed there do to the fact that I had a convulsion back at my apartment. He said that I told him on the highway that I was headed to my girlfriends. I denied it. They finally agreed to bring me to the hospital. I told the doctor that I usually receive a shot of valium after a seizure. They said no go and the officer tried to convince me to have a blood test to prove my sobriety. I told them that no one puts a needle in my arm for no good dam reason. Nothing gained, nothing accomplished. They wanted some hard evidence to convict me. Since I went into a blackout, not knowing what I was doing, I considered myself not guilty.

Well, to make a long story short, I got sentenced to sixty days in the House of Correction. What a fucking bummer. I lost my license for five years, and if it wasn't for that I was living in the heart of Boston, I probably would have been dead by now.

Well it turned out to be another day in the life. What happened several years ago is like what you would consider a bad case of amnesia. You think that you have been floating on cloud nine. And in one way that's where you've been. But in another way, you think of all the positive aspects you've achieved.

If Hunter Thompson were here right now, he'd say it was all a kindergarten.

The judicial system sucks. What more could you say? The fascist regime is rising. Pull over. They want to see where you're at, where you're going, just more or less. The wife expected you home an hour ago. Better off staying in and get feeling good at home. Well let's not get too heavy on this small bit because a taste of some alcohol, or, whatever would do fine right now.

I'm going back to the day when the government turned up the voltage slowly but surely on me eight years ago and everything that happened to cause this obstacle is coming back to me like it was yesterday.

Here I am waiting to go on my vacation (sixty days in the House of Correction), for supposedly drunk driving (what does the system know?). I ran into some dude that knew of the people that had me do the time I did previously. We were both awaiting the paddy wagon to do our bids, so we decided to shoot the breeze.

He was originally from Reading, Mass and he knew a few of my former bros from the Evil Spirits MC. And he started explaining to me where he knew of me. He told me that he was at the party Jumpin' Jack held for the Halloween of '74. It turned out to be one hell of a party. We went on and on and started talking about the party that happened a week after that, and how another former bro of the Spirits took the credit for the stabbing that happened there, which was self defense I used, and did the time for it. He ran into Zap a while ago from doing time with him. I knew Zap was a liar, but this really pissed me off. That was the start of my flashback experiences.

In any event, the day went on and everything seemed not to be an accident. Facts not fiction, so it goes, so it goes. A guard took all the data down and directed me to the medical infirmary. The nurse asked me what type of medication I took and told me that I couldn't take my tranquilizers, just my other type of anti-convulsive that I had.

She explained to me that I should talk to their psychiatrist, "We had a problem with an epileptic here before when he created a riot with the prisoners."

"Yeah," I said while not thinking of anything that happened in the past.

She went on. "He'd have a fit and a fight would break out because of the way he acted."

I didn't think much of it. "Well, this is from a head injury, I wasn't born with epilepsy," I explained.

"I can't give you your tranquilizers. They're not allowed in here. Fights break out over them with other inmates," she said.

"Hey, look, I'm not worried about anyone hassling me. How are they going to know anyway? And even if they do, they're not going to get anywhere with me on my meds," I spoke up.

She went on, "Look, you have to see the doctor before anything can be affirmed. We would have you do your sentencing at the Bridgewater State Mental Institution with your condition. We can't take any chances with what happened before with an epileptic, and at the same time you would be able to take your meds," she persisted.

So I stayed in the hospital setting for the weekend. The minute I'm walking through the gate an old friend I met in this jail eight years ago was standing in the gateway. "Hey, Parco, what brings you here?" he asked.

"Hey, Joe, what's up? How come you're in the infirmary?" I wondered.

"I'm leaving tomorrow. The fuckin' screws did a number on me, just for the hell of it, as a goin' away present. The fuckin' goon squad," he said sarcastically.

"Figures, they probably don't want your ass back here, so they're givin' you a hint," I said wisely.

Joey went on talking about old times that happened either in the jail or with the people we both knew from the City of Lawrence. He didn't know where he was going when he got out the next day so I told him that I'd contact a friend that could put him up for a week. I went to the pay phone and gave him a ring. The answer was yes and he could stay for a week without any problems.

So Joey kept on talkin' about past experiences. Remember this, that, and another thing, remember, remember. He kept on bringing up the bullshit that I really didn't give a fuck about, but I tried to listen intently. Everything seemed to be a puzzle to me and I had to back track my mind to focus on the pieces that were missing to get the frame assembled to bring the picture to a noticeable abstract inside my head.

I finally put one and one together, and how the riot went on in here the time I was here in the past and it hit me like a jolt inside my head, telling me that I was the epileptic that caused the incident. How everything progressed from the day I was incarcerated in '77, not getting my proper medication from the beginning, to fighting off the faggots that I didn't want to have anything to do with. Who drove me crazy with their obsessional thoughts, building up my own reputation among other inmates who respected me for not giving in to the way the system was operating. How the House ended up going through a shake-down for drugs being hidden due to the way I expressed myself to that certain nurse that I just saw when I ran into her the first time I was here and how she took my thoughts seriously on how the joint was operating—like a fuckin' animal zoo. And the assholes who were running the system didn't give a fuck except for their paychecks. Here I was still recovering from a brain operation, that wasn't even completed with a protective plate I was going to have as a finishing touch. And I had to have these assholes screw me up worse than when I first came in.

I could go on and on about how the inmates decided to riot and tear the house apart due to the reversed psychology I used, but I don't have to. For the answer which I am trying to reveal is best expressed by the events of the next day. It was then I saw that nurse again. She was one who initiated me in for the second time. I was there for a stupid driving under the influence charge, which was due to the impact of my head injury and indulging in alcohol to kill the pain. She ran into my past file and she looked at me like the cat got her tongue. I got the impression from her that if I kept my mouth shut, she'd keep hers shut. And so the merry-go-round went inside my head, figuring that there was no sense even telling anyone what happened due to the extreme paranoia I was experiencing because they would not giving me my correct medication in the first place. Why bother creating some more trouble with the fact that I'd really crack up this time and it would be Bridgewater, here I come, or locked-up permanently for the time I had to do. No way! Not this man! And so I did the time on cloud one-hundred-nine with the flashbacks immersing inside my head, the ozone so to speak. Not knowing whether I'd maintain or what. Just minute by minute so to speak.

Thank God the day came that it was time to roll out of that joint and the first thing that was handed to me was my medication that I was unable to take for the sixty days. Boy it felt great to get back to the outside world. But the flashbacks were still creeping up in me. Voices I heard in the house still haunt me. The system sucks. What can I say?

22

The Bad Times Roll

Dude went on his own after the club completely dismantled. He headed down to Florida and worked as a miner. During the early eighties there was a union trucking strike across the country. At that time, independent truckers were doing the work of the union drivers. They were getting shot while driving by snipers, since they were interfering with the union strike. Dude was one of those drivers during that strike.

The story I read in the Lawrence newspaper stated that Arthur Williams (Dude) was on a run and was making a stop in Texas. He met a couple at a bar, got friendly, and talked about the strike. He explained to them that he was going to complete his run whether or not there were any snipers along his trip. The couple invited him over to their apartment. When they arrived, a game of Russian Roulette was brought forth. Game over! Dude supposedly pulled the trigger and lodged a bullet in his brain. When I read the article I thought, this can't be true! Dude might have been a crazy fucker, but not crazy enough to risk his own life in that sense. When I attended the wake, I spoke with his former wife who had two of his children. She had the same notion as I did, that he was shot and killed and a cover-up was implicated. A northerner doesn't fit in that southern hospitality. Knowing Dude, with his rowdy, loud-mouthed attitude, I wouldn't have doubted that he was set up and murdered. He had more balls then brains, but he did have a head on his shoulders. God rest his soul.

One of the former brother's Jean Lemieux wound up going big time into the drug cartel with the cocaine business. He was dealing from Florida to Canada connecting with the Hell's Angels. Massachusetts was one of his stepping stones during the ordeal. These leg wetting facts from these newspaper articles will give you the low down on what took place in a multi-million dollar enterprise.

DRUG RING WINDS ITS WAY FROM COLUMBIA TO VALLEY
Dec.11, 1988

The federal probe into a $200 million cocaine ring in southern New Hampshire and Greater Lawrence may hinge on two shadowy drug and gun runners with ties to Colombia's notorious Medellin drug cartel and the Hell's Angels in Canada.

Robert LeClerc of Quebec, Canada, and Coconut Grove, Fla., and Brian Riberdy, 9 Walnut Terrace, Salem, N.H., got long prison sentences in Miami after pleading guilty to gun and drug charges in March 1987. While neither man is charged here, their ties to the New Hampshire case-particularly reputed ringleader Jean Marie Lemieux of Salem, N.H.-are striking.

Both cases stretch from Florida to Canada, with New Hampshire as a key link.

Key Witnesses?

Defendants in the drug case believe Mr. Riberdy and Mr. LeClerc are the government's main witnesses against them. But New Hampshire prosecutors refuse to answer questions about the men and whether they are informants.

"I have no intention of exposing the identity of the witnesses at this point," said Assistant U.S. Attorney for New Hampshire, Robert McDaniel.

Stephen Morreale, spokesman for the federal Drug Enforcement Administration in Boston, would neither confirm nor deny the involvement of Mr. Riberdy and Mr. LeClerc in the New Hampshire probe, but said the Eagle-Tribune should "keep digging" and "continue in that vein."

Both Mr. LeClerc and Mr. Riberdy show signs of being protected federal witnesses. Neither man is registered in federal prison-despite getting long sentences only a year ago.

Ramsey Bahrawy, lawyer for Julian Dupont, who now lives in a Salem duplex where Mr. Riberdy used to live, said most of the 21 defendants think Mr. Riberdy and Mr. LeClerc are the sources of the government's charges.

Mr. Bahrawy accused prosecutors of intimidating his client by holding him without bail-so he will break down and testify against the suspected kingpins-Mr. Lemieux and Carlos Arboleda, 2 Canal St., Lawrence.

"Their information from LeClerc and Riberdy isn't enough," Mr. Bahrawy said. "They need someone from inside. They're trying to get him in the hopes that he spills his guts."

Prosecutors would not comment on that accusation, but acknowledged pressuring defendants to testify is common practice in conspiracy cases.

The Hells Angels Connection

Last year, when Mr. Riberdy was sentenced, Assistant U.S. Attorney in Miami Steven Chaykin told the Eagle-Tribune the Salem man was trying to smuggle an anti-tank gun and other weapons to the Canadian Hell's Angels for assassinations.

The infamous motorcycle gang was known in the 1960s for long hair, leather and a tendency toward violence. Angel "security guards" killed a man at the Rolling Stones' concert at Altamont Speedway in California in 1969.

But in the 1980s, the Hell's Angels throughout America had grown into a sophisticated gang of machine-gun-toting well-dressed organized criminals who made millions dealing drugs.

Federal agents made a big move on them in 1985. That was also a landmark year for Hell's Angels in Canada.

Constable Mark Richer of the Royal Canadian Mounted Police in Quebec said the group became "an out-of-control drug distributor" until five Hell's Angels were murdered and dumped in the St. Lawrence River in 1985.

"They are affiliated with other clubs in the U.S. along the same line of activities," he said.

South American Drug Cartel

According to a federal indictment handed down in Florida against them last year, Mr. LeClerc and Mr. Riberdy conspired to run machine guns, silencers, rocket launchers and grenades for the Miami area from an unknown date until Feb. 5, 1987.

Mr. Riberdy was sentenced to five years. Mr. LeClerc-also convicted in 1987 of other arms dealing charges, reportedly with the murderous multibillion-dollar Medellin cocaine cartel in Colombia-got a total of 33 years in prison.

Time magazine reported in February 1987 that the Medellin cartel is "a powerful crime cabal that is said to supply 80 percent of the world's cocaine. The group rakes in billions of dollars annually, allegedly smuggling up to 15 tons of cocaine monthly into the U.S. and Europe."

The cartel reportedly employs house assassins, controls most police in the country to protect its lucrative operation, and has turned Colombia into a war zone.

The cartel is blamed in the murders of policemen, judges and journalists, and the government is failing to put them out of business.

Acting U.S. Attorney for New Hampshire Peter E. Papps was asked last week whether the Granite State drug operation was involved with the Medellin cartel, as the cocaine came from Colombia.

"We're not saying it's just the Medellin cartel," he said.

Who are LeClerc, Riberdy?

Who are these two mystery figures?

Mr. LeClerc is named as a co-conspirator in the New Hampshire drug probe and figures prominently in the 28-charge, 52-page indictment unsealed last week after authorities arrested 21 defendants in New Hampshire, Massachusetts, Florida and Canada.

Although he is not a defendant, one of many allegations against Mr. LeClerc is that he smuggled 1,450 kilograms of cocaine into the U.S. from Colombia in the last three months of 1984 and was a major supplier in Florida to Mr. Lemieux, who is also originally from Canada.

Mr. LeClerc has been in the United States for about eight years, according to Royal Canadian Mounted Police records in Canada. Mr. Lemieux has been in the United States since at least 1982.

Mr. Riberdy, Mr. LeClerc's gun-running partner in Florida, was also Mr. Lemieux's friend and next-door neighbor in Salem.

He lived in one half of a duplex at 9-11 Walnut Terrace, Salem, N.H., that police say Mr. Lemieux bought with drug money and used to complete drug deals.

The Day The Bust Began

Feb. 5, 1987, may be the most important day in this tale.

First it was the day Mr. Riberdy and Mr. LeClerc walking into an arrest federal investigators had been planning since August 1986.

And it was the day federal authorities began to unravel the sophisticated drug operation they allege Mr. Lemieux, Mr. Arboleda and their co-defendants were running.

The suspected New Hampshire drug conspirators walked unknowingly into the same trap.

The drug indictment alleges three things happened Feb. 5, 1987:

First, Mr. LeClerc tried to possess with the intent to distribute 105 kilograms of cocaine.

Second, Mr. Lemieux discussed the purchase of automatic weapons, plastic explosives and handheld rockets that day.

Third Mr. LeClerc conducted a meeting of the purpose of consummating a cocaine transaction within New Hampshire.

It was their last such discussion.

Acting U.S. Attorney Mr. Papps refused to say whom Mr. Lemieux discussed buying the weapons with, but the indictment suggests he was talking with Mr. LeClerc.

Mr. Chaykins said Mr. Riberdy, who was living next door to Mr. Lemieux at the time, made several trips from Salem to Florida to meet with Mr. LeClerc, who owned a sport shop in Coconut Grove.

An undercover agent and confidential informant arranged to sell Mr. Riberdy and Mr. LeClerc the weapons for $29,000. The transaction was videotaped by federal authorities.

According to the drug indictments, cocaine dealing between Mr. LeClerc and Mr. Lemieux goes back to 1982, when they established and operated a stash house for drugs at 243 West Newton St. in Boston's Back Bay.

That same year, Mr. Lemieux bought a fully automatic MAC-11 machine gun equipped with a silencer for $3,000, the indictment says.

From September through December 1984, Mr. LeClerc allegedly imported 1,450 kilograms of cocaine from Colombia and sold Mr. Lemieux 80 kilograms.

That same year, the indictment alleges they recruited and paid Christian B. Poirier and Michael Patey to "mule" cocaine from southern Florida to New Hampshire.

During the first three months of 1985, Mr. Lemieux allegedly bought six shipments of cocaine in southern Florida, each between five and eight kilograms, and another 10 kilograms that June.

In July 1986, Richard Rousseau of Quebec allegedly drove five kilograms of cocaine from Florida to New Hampshire.

On Nov. 26, 1986, Mr. Lemieux allegedly met with Mr. LeClerc in New York City at the Plaza Hotel, a time when he and co-conspirators agreed to step up their drug activity to shipping 40 kilograms a month to New Hampshire in 10-killogram installments.

On Dec. 3, 1986, Mr. Rousseau allegedly shipped another 10 kilograms of cocaine from Florida to New Hampshire.

Where are they?

Authorities in the New Hampshire case refused to disclose the current whereabouts of Mr. Riberdy and Mr. LeClerc.

According to Bureau of Prisons in Florida, Mr. LeClerc has been in "prolonged transit" in the custody of U.S. marshals since March 18, 1988.

Mr. Riberdy was released from the Metropolitan Correctional Center in Miami to the U.S. Marshal's Service Aug. 8, 1987, only three months after he was sentenced, according to the prison bureau.

If the men had been sentenced to another federal prison, the bureau's computer would list them.

That means they are probably still in the custody of the U.S. marshals and being used as informants, an official at the bureau said.

"My guess is, they're protecting them," the official said. "It's customary. There's a good reason why you can't find them."

Daryl Williams, a spokesman for the U. S. Customs Service in Miami, said he could not find the status of the two prisoners.

But he had an idea.

"It sounds to me like a strong possibility that they're cooperating with the government," he said. "And they could appear as witnesses at the trial."

"Reprinted courtesy of The Salem News"

SALEM MAN ACCUSED OF BEING KINGPIN MAKES $100,000 BAIL Dec.23, 1988

Concord, N.H.-The man who authorities say headed an international drug ring has made bail of $100,000 cash and now must report to a probation officer thrice weekly, among other strict bail conditions.

Jean Marie Lemieux, 34, a Canadian citizen living in Salem, was bailed out of state prison yesterday at about 3 p.m., a U.S. District Court spokeswoman said.

His release was cleared Monday when U.S. District Judge Shane Devine rejected the U.S. attorney's argument that he should be held without bail. Mr. Devine upheld a federal magistrate's decision to set bail at $100,000 cash and $250,000 unsecured bond.

Under the order, Mr. Lemieux must restrict his travel to New Hampshire and Massachusetts, report to the probation office three times a week, submit to urine analyses, get a job and refrain from use of alcohol and drugs and possession of guns and other weapons.

Mr. Lemieux has been charged with 16 counts of trafficking and faces two life sentences if convicted.

He was among 21 people from Canada, New Hampshire, Massachusetts and Florida indicted on drug trafficking and conspiracy charges in a drug sweep federal authorities have called the largest ever in New England. The ring imported more than 2,310 pounds of cocaine worth $200 million, authorities said.

A trial date has been set for Feb. 7.

"Reprinted courtesy of The Salem News"

Just being out on bail for a couple of days, Jean dug $120,000 out of his backyard, wrapped it in Christmas paper, headed to Boston to bribe a government witness. Federal agents seized the cash at the Logan Airport Hilton Hotel. Jean admitted it was "proceeds of narcotics trafficking," according to a court document. The Federal drug enforcement officials and Salem N.H. police used a backhoe to search for money in his backyard. Nothing was found. He eventually became one of the top government informants and hardly did any time in prison over the situation.

After the 74 murder of the two Hell's Angels I knew, the all out war was still escalating. Here is a newspaper clipping from the mid 90's.

EXPECTED BIKER RUMBLE FIZZLES July 31, 1995

After a weekend of murder and wild freeway shootouts, a show-down between rival gangs fizzled out yesterday in Brockton.

State and local police showed up in force at an outdoor concert in Brockton, where the Hell's Angels, Outlaws and Devil's Disciples were expected to rumble.

Two Devil's Disciples members were attacked Saturday afternoon, and one died. Bikers called it a turf war and predicted more violence was coming.

"If it comes, it won't be bang bang, it'll be all out," said one brawny biker outside the Brockton concert. "They were telling me it was dangerous even for me to go."

Another biker at the concert said, "It's all over turf, and they're not going to stop. Not 'til one of them takes control."

Two gun-toting Hell's Angels were still on the loose yesterday, after they rammed a rival Disciple in Weymouth Saturday and dragged him 400 feet along Route 18, police said.

The biker, William Michaels, 45, of Londonderry, H.H., was killed in the attack, police said.

The rival gang member's Cadillac then crashed into another car, and the two thugs ran away from the car, police said.

Inside the red DeVille was a wad of cash, along with a police scanner and two cellular phones, leading police to believe drugs may have been a motive.

After the crash, one of the men ran off into thick brush and disappeared.

The other, waving a gun, accosted a couple in a Dodge Sprint, forced them out and drove off, police said.

The car was found later in a Friendly's restaurant parking lot in South Weymouth. Police believe the bearded, tattooed man drove off in a Ford Taurus.

A few minutes before the 3 p.m. attack in Weymouth, other Disciples got into a wild shoot-out with a van on Interstate 93 in Quincy.

Pocked with bullets, the van veered off the highway, and four men ran away, police said.

One Disciple, Shade Dadeau, 20, of Manchester N.H., was shot in the chest, but is expected to recover. He was under tight security last night at Boston City Hospital.

"The bikers are the same story as the Mafia," said Weymouth Detective Capt. Rod Rumble. "Back in the '60s, they were disciplined. Now they'll do anything. They're a ruthless group."

Rumble said the FBI had warned the Weymouth police of possible biker violence this weekend because of biker gatherings in the area.

A gang source said the Devil's Disciples have joined forces with the Outlaws to take over territory claimed by the Hell's Angels.

"Reprinted with permission of the Boston Herald"

Another local bust takes place on the Lynn, Massachusetts Hell's Angels M.C. Here is the newspaper write-up.

15 HELD IN HELLS ANGELS DRUG BUST Oct.6, 1996

During a series of predawn raids yesterday morning, heavily armed law enforcement agents stormed into a Lynn neighborhood in an armored personnel carrier to arrest the East Coast chairman of the Hell's Angels motorcycle gang on drug charges.

Just after 5:30 a.m., federal, state and local police barged past a dozen chained pit bulls at the gang's fortified clubhouse and seized computers, fax machines and business records of what law enforcement authorities called one of the major distribution networks for cocaine and methamphetamine on the North Shore.

During the raids, law enforcement agents arrested 15 members or associates of the Salem chapter of the Hell's Angels, including Gregory Domey, 36, of Lynn, former president of the Salem chapter and the reputed head of the East Coast branch of the Hell's Angels. The 15, along with one other who was not arrested yesterday, were charged with conspiracy to distribute cocaine or methamphetamine.

Alluding to the arrests last week of the Intervale Street gang in Boston on drug charges and the arrests earlier this year of members of the Diablo motorcycle gang in Springfield-also the result of coordinated efforts by various law enforcement agencies-US Attorney Donald K. Stern said joint investigations are paying off.

"This case represents another step in a concerted effort on the part of federal, state and local law enforcement to specifically target violent organizations, particularly when they traffic in drugs and use violence, threats and intimidation as part of their stock in trade," Stern said at a morning news conference announcing the arrests.

During searches of 10 locations including Sin City Cycles, the Lynn motorcycle shop managed by Domey, law enforcement agents seized eight guns, more than $20,000 in cash and a half-pound of cocaine.

Building on an investigation begun in the fall of 1994 by the Massachusetts State Police into alleged drug trafficking by Michael R. Quintiliani, 24 of Wakefield, the US Drug Enforcement Administration used an informant to make more than 40 undercover drug purchases from Domey and associates, according to an affidavit filed in US District Court.

During one five-hour period on Feb. 21, the undercover DEA agent arranged to pick up 30 ouches of cocaine in 3-ounce increments. The deliveries were made at half-hour intervals in the parking lots of various well-known spots along Route 1, including the Hilltop Restaurant, Hockey Town, Weylu's Restaurant and TGI Friday's. In all, the DEA made $200,000 worth of drug buys during the 18-month period, according to DEA special agent in charge George C. Festa.

Security was particularly tight at US District Court, where the 15 were held without bail by Chief Magistrate Judge Marianne B. Bowler pending detention hearings Tuesday.

As defendants were escorted into the courthouse, state troopers with machine guns guarded the entryway. And when they were brought into the courtroom, troopers formed a phalanx behind them.

In addition to Domey and Quintiliani, also arrested were: Christopher Rainieri, 28, Erich Gunderman, 36, and Scott Brackett, 30, all of Lynn; David Witham, 33, of Saugus; John Battista, 31, and Anthony Serino, 29, both of

Revere; John R. Bartolomeo, 27, of East Boston; George Currier J. of Revere; Andrew Deleary, 37, Anthony Eicks, 30, and Sean Barr, 31, all of Lynn; and John Conway, 39, and Michael Kearney, 40, both of East Boston.

A 16th defendant, David Gunderman, 36, of Lynn, is still being sought.

Stern said the Salem chapter of Hell's Angels, headquartered in a red wooden house down the street from Domey's house, had taken over the cul-de-sac where Domey and several associates lived.

"This area," said Stern, holding up an aerial view of the Shaw's Court neighborhood, "was basically controlled by the Hell's Angels." He described the clubhouse as an armed fortress guarded at all times by gun toting members and pit bulls. Inside the clubhouse, video cameras and 10 monitors tracked activity.

Outside the three-story Victorian that served as the gang's clubhouse yesterday, several motorcycles were parked in the fenced-in yard. Three security cameras were trained on the front door.

Authorities said the arrests were particularly significant because the group was a major source for methamphetamine, a drug whose popularity has spread from California to the Midwest. So far it has been largely absent in Massachusetts, authorities said.

Two affidavits filed in court described the Hell's Angels as the largest outlaw motorcycle gang in the world, with more than 1,200 members in the United States and 600 in foreign countries. Traditionally, according to law enforcement officials, drug trafficking has been its main source of income.

Domey, the East Coast leader, is a celebrity of sorts. He and his Harley-Davidson appeared on the cover of a Scandinavian motorcycle magazine last fall and he appeared as a Hell's Angel in Robert DeNiro's movie, "A Bronx Tale."

The affidavits also suggest that the Salem gang may be tied to violence involving rival motorcycle gangs: the Devil's Disciples and the Outlaws. On July 29, 1995, a Devil's Disciple was run down and killed in Weymouth and on June 20 of this year three members of the Outlaws were shot in Brockton.

While the criminal charges filed yesterday do not include either of those incidents, Stern said the investigation is continuing.

"Reprinted with permission from www.copyright.com"

After so many motorcycle accidents, fights, double dealings and rip off, Zap put himself six feet under. I was told by a former H.A. member that he got dishonorably discharged from the club. He was caught ripping off some money from the entertainment business that the Angels were involved in. It expanded from the west coast to Europe. Once out of the club, he wound up back in jail do to some domestic violence he was convicted of. After doing time, I was told that he got involved in shooting up dope and overdosed himself to the happy hunting ground. All and all, I didn't know how to feel when I heard the news. I introduced him to the biker world, and what he did was screw his own brothers. He was hurting anyway from all the broken bones he accumulated. Well, it's like the old saying, what goes around, comes around. Maybe he paid himself back for his own ignorance. As the late brother Dude use to state, "You Lose, Ha, Ha, Ha!"

I decided to take a ride on my scoot through the Merrimack Valley, which is my original stomping grounds, following the Merrimack River. I've been living for about three years, Salisbury Beach that is, where the mouth of the river recedes. I had a lot of strange and wild vibrations as I buzzed through Lowell, the former city where my father started his restaurant business. Everything looked illuminated, since everything was new. Boston University built an extension a few miles away. Modern technology was everywhere. The site of the restaurant that I helped built reminded me of an old Humphrey Bogart scene, people playing pool, while others were laid back eating and drinking. Right in the back, where I used to trail ride were all different cooperate greed heads. I decided to case the area a couple of times, since I use to trail ride out here. After that it was back toward downtown Lowell, right by the corner of 2nd St. at Duncan Donuts for an ice coffee on a hot summer night. I ran into a couple of regulars from the area and new of the Angels that I knew of from the 70's, ho, ho, ho. I got word of the old bros that I was associated with. I already heard that Mousey died of a heart failure years ago. Fuck-Up was so banged up from the injuries that he sustained that the bros thought twice of letting him back into the club, plus, it is said that it is rare for a second shot into the club if you were already once a member. I was hearing all strange stories how Suave Dave got killed till I heard that evening, that it was his former or present ol'lady that snuffed him with a bullet and was found not guilty. Next I was told that Hook was doing time for some environmental protection scam. He was involved in illegally dumping toxic waste in the area he was operating out of. Hawkeye was out working as a land clearer, cutting trees and that sort of bit. What a small world life can bring you. The tide always returns from where it derived from.

My drinking days are finished, but when I look back at them I learned that in old school the idea is "keeping the glass half full." It can go as far as poor me, poor me, pour me another drink type attitude. I just don't know. I just don't know. What I do know is looking back into plowing into a fire hydrant with Dude's Oldsmobile in the middle of winter was another experience. I was stoned on downs and alcohol. Taking Dennis's car into a telephone pole was a boozed-narcotic experience. I was with a chick that was twice as stoned as me and she was reaching for the steering wheel, telling me to stay to left and stay to the right and then bang! I settled with a DUI conviction on a .07 breath count. Innocent by the book! Totaling Preacher's car right into a guardrail down cemetery hill not even a 500 yards from the clubhouse with his expression when I just walked back through the door was "man I thought you just left."

It was a combination of traumatic brain injuries along with drugs and alcohol that blew my fuse. I could go on and on about how I survived through this whole ordeal, but all I can say was that the lord and the devil were both with me right through the whole procession. I leave it at that!

23

Conclusion

Well, I finally come back to the conclusion that nothing is sacred, only the dead are living. When you have made it over the edge and survived, you will know what I mean! The hang-around that could have been, wannabe-didn't cut it. The "had to be" were the ones that lived it truly. They are the ones in a separate entity through living on the edge from reality to insanity, and back to surface level. Experiences such as wild sex-fights-drugs, and naturally, motorcycles were the scene. Nothing is an accident ... everything has a reason, only obstacles we have to avoid. Ignorance or enlightenment—they are both the same thing. The solution is to keep it in the middle way and correct the wrong doings in life. Living on the edge is a dangerous way of getting fucked over in the end, by injury, incarceration or death. These would be some of your obstacles which you must master to avoid. Richness on the spiritual plane is abundant. I turned out to be a loner. I'm on a different level now.

I'll always be in favor of the Hell's Angels no matter what the circumstance is. A lot of members got a raw deal such as an unavoidable obstacle they were confronted with. That is similar to the deaths of R.B. and Whiskey George that happened in 74 with the Outlaw M.C. That confrontation turned out to be an all out gang war which is still brewing today. A lot of killings have occurred since that slaying. Flying colors today is like watching your back from ether side, law or outlaw. Well, I don't want to get to heavy into this bit since life will always roll on. It rolls on a Harley Davidson. That's what keeps me going. When I look back at the club years, everything seemed to move in synchrony. Like I stated before, nothing is an accident. Now I realize that everything happened for a reason. We caused the majority of our problems on our own. We were too far out of it to realize the obstacles we had to face. After my operation and completely finished with my legal problems, I went into doing my own rehabilitation. While I did my time in 77 for the bum rap I mentioned, I started to do my writing. The first draft of this book was written in prison! I went to Adult Education in the mid

80's for short story writing. I saw the late Dr Hunter S Thompson speak at a lecture at Somerville Theatre. I have read all his works, and consider him one of my idols. In 78, I started working out everyday, from weight lifting to running from 5 to 10 miles and working out on the heavy boxing bag doing 10 rounds in one workout. I continued for 15 yrs. I also got involved into meditation. In 83, I became a Buddhist member. We chant the Lotus Sutra to our Gohonzon, which is similar to a scroll. That takes about an hour in the morning and the same in the evening. I was able to accomplish on emptying the mind. I also got into practicing zazen. That is a sitting, breathing technique. By practicing these techniques faithfully, you will reach the paranormal, believe me. I worked on sobriety which was a demon to it's self. I started getting involved in politics and started working for the public sector. I made it up on Beacon Hill in Boston to work for the Attorney General's Office. It was an experience to it's self. I was doing my workout and meditations at the same time. I felt like the Terminator, it was like living on your second wind, or then again, your second attention. But everything seems to take its place on the right path. I got into the main stream of "spoken word" in the metropolitan Boston and did some readings also in San Francisco and N.Y.C. I'm still riding a Harley and talking to my brother Snake who moved back up to Canada. We still talk about old times like it just happened yesterday. But he's doing it and still riding. All the brothers are far apart now, but close in spirit. Ah yes, Evil Spirits that is!

Ah, but I was so much older then,
I'm younger than that now.

—Bob Dylan, My Back Pages

About the Author

Parco Senia, born in Lawrence, Massachusetts, became a juvenile delinquent at age 12. A life threatening injury, suffered during his biker years, eventually led him to the wisdom of Buddhism and Hunter S. Thompson. He daily rides his Harley up the seacoast. Parco currently lives in Salisbury, Massachusetts, where he enjoys writing and walking the beach daily.

978-0-595-45969-8
0-595-45969-2